QUEEN

A KIND OF MAGIC

AN ILLUSTRATED HISTORY

By Michael O'Neill

Danann
BOOKS

Danann
BOOKS

First Published Danann Publishing Ltd 2018

CAT NO: DAN0393

Photography courtesy of

Getty images:

Michael Putland	Georges De Keerle
Mark and Colleen Hayward	Steve Wood / Stringer
RB/Redferns	Ebet Roberts/Redferns
Fin Costello/Redferns	Dave Hogan
Koh Hasebe/Shinko Music	David Redfern/Redferns
Anwar Hussein	Patrick AVENTURIER/Gamma-Rapho
Michael Ochs Archives / Stringer	Brian Rasic
Waring Abbott	FG/Bauer-Griffin
Richard E. Aaron	John Rodgers/Redferns

Other images Wiki Commons

Book layout & design Darren Grice at Ctrl-d

Copy Editor Tom O'Neill

Made in EU.

ISBN: 978-1-912332-22-9

CONTENTS

INTRODUCTION

"*I*t's a bird, it's a plane, it's Superman!" enthuse the characters in the 1966 Superman musical. For music fans the world over, the astonishment would surely be rephrased to read, *"It's a rock group, it's a fantastical musical hall act, it's indescribable, it's Queen!"*

Even before the moment when Queen burst into the awareness of the international record-buying public with Bohemian Rhapsody in 1975, they had taken the music industry by the scruff of the neck and whirled it around their heads with gleeful abandon, breaking pop music 'rules' by the dozen as they went, with Freddie Mercury strutting the stage like an animated multicoloured ship's figurehead on speed, hurling the waves aside as he went where no vocal chords had dared go before.

Queen — the original successful line up was Freddie Mercury, Brian May, Roger Taylor and John Deacon — dived into every genre of music they could find and retrieved anything that would help them to deliver the sound, the diversity, the rainbow panorama and the success they wanted for their music. From music hall to metal, from Michael Jackson to ragtime, from camp to Caribbean, Brian May's guitar virtuosity swirled around Freddie Mercury's extraordinary vocal dexterity to produce sounds never heard before or since as they and their legions of fans revelled in the sheer exuberance of their performances. Theatrically combining mock opera and quasi-classical elements, Queen's kitschy humour and exaggerated style was built upon a rock-solid musical foundation; the group was an amalgam of sharp talents and each band member composed many hit songs.

But Queen's shining comet was to blaze for just over 20 years; it came crashing to a tragic end with the death of their charismatic frontman in 1991. Without Freddie Mercury's mercurial personality and his unique voice soaring into the clouds, the world of music could never quite be the same again. His flamboyance, musical and personal courage had catapulted the group to the pinnacle of world success, his irrepressible nature made them one of the most popular groups on the planet. Not a bad epitaph for a boy of Indian descent who started out life in Tanzania as Farrokh "*Freddie*" Bulsara and said farewell to it as the shining light in the...

... RADIANT MUSICAL PHENOMENA THAT WAS KNOWN AS QUEEN.

ABOVE: Queen portraits, 1973 - Clockwise from top Left:
Freddie Mercury; Roger Taylor; John Deacon; Brian May

The Queen story begins, explodes, and moves into popular music legend with the life of one man, Freddie Mercury, whose parents, at the time of his birth, were Parsee Indians living in Zanzibar, now part of Tanzania, where Farrokh Bulsara saw the light of day on the 5th of September 1946 in Zanzibar City on the main island of Unguja, Father Bomi and mother Jer, were Zoroastrians, and once he had undergone a ritual bathing ceremony, the baby Farrokh became one, too, and remained so throughout his life. Bomi was a senior civil servant, which meant that Farrokh's family had the advantage of a good standard of living, employing domestic staff and a nanny. In later life, perhaps ever wary of being an outsider in his adopted country, the future Freddie Mercury would always approach questions about his young life with cautious restraint bordering on irritation, so that many details still remain obscure.

The first and least dramatic in a series of changes to this smooth early life came when Farrokh was five and sent to attend the local missionary school. Who amongst his family and relatives could have known that as he piped his songs for them at that early age, they were listening to a future musical star?

Who could have known, either, that not far behind Farrokh in age, having been born in July 1947, another boy making his five-year-old journey to his first school, Hanworth Road primary school in London, would join up with Freddie to form one of the greatest rock groups in the world. And coincidently, the house that Brian Harold May was born and lived in was very close to the one that the Bulsara's would inhabit in London in later years.

Brian's talent in music was given a step up when his father Harold taught him a few chords on the ukulele, which then lead to piano lessons, and when he was seven years old — fortunately, and despite that fact that money was scarce, his father seemed more in tune with what might interest his son than many other parents — an acoustic guitar appeared in his bedroom.

And it was father Harold who propelled Brian even further into the world of pop music when he brought home a record of 'Rock Island Line' by Lonnie Donegan. There was no going back for Brian, and he was now firmly caught in the net cast out by Buddy Holly, Little Richard, the Everly Brothers and his first unattainable love, Connie Francis. He spent his pocket money on records, proving to be a punctilious collector of all things from matchboxes to comics. And it was around this time that he also got caught in the fascinating web of astronomy thanks to TV presenter Patrick Moore. From then on, music and science would pour their delights into his life in tandem, but while he was at school, he applied himself rigorously to his studies.

Whilst Freddie and Brian were already out in the world, in an English county to the north-east of London, West Norfolk, the next piece of the Queen puzzle had to wait until the 26th of July 1949 to start his journey to stardom. And just a few years later, he was moved even further away from the musical spark plug that was London, after a sister was born in 1953 and the family moved down to Cornwall in the very south-west of England. Roger Meddows Taylor was then sent off to Bosvigo school in the town of Truro, where the family were living.

Music filled his ears during his early life from his mother's accordion, and by the age of eight, Roger had started playing the ukulele, which he enjoyed so much that just a couple of months later he formed a skiffle group called the Bubblingover Boys. Using instruments that were either homemade or improvised — a washboard, kazoo, tea-chest bass, comb and paper or cigar-box fiddle — together with the ukulele and guitars, they were 'terrible, really terrible', and soon broke up.

Two years later still, in August 1951, at St. Francis' private hospital in Leicester, Lillian and Arthur Deacon became proud parents of little boy. They called him John Richard. Almost twenty years exactly would pass before John Richard's life would be turned on its head. John's sister, Julie, was born five years later, and they led a comfortable and uneventful life, with 'Deaks' or 'Deaky' as he was known to his friends, attending Linden Junior School in Leicester. But tragedy struck when John was just ten years old; their father died.

The family moved to Oadby, a small town to the south-east of Leicester, and John's next school was Gartree High School followed by Beauchamp Grammar School. He was aged 14 when he joined the band Opposition playing rhythm guitar for their covers of chart hits, switching to bass the following year. Apart from his growing interest in soul music, electronics was John's consuming interest.

In keeping with his other future bandmates, the young Deacon was an extremely good scholar, and when he left school, he had eight GCE O levels and three grade A, A-level passes in his pocket. By 1969, when the band had renamed themselves Art, and John had accepted a place at Chelsea Art College, his days in the band were over. (When he left college in 1971, he had gained a first class degree in Electronics.)

Meanwhile, Farrokh had been joined by a baby sister, Kashmira, who was born in 1952; but a far greater upheaval to his life came in 1955. Deciding that their precocious son, a term Freddie used about himself, would get a better education at boarding school in India, the eight-year-old boy was sent off alone to the subcontinent and St. Peter's Boys School in Panchgani and a new life in the present-day state of Maharashtra.

Farrokh appeared to enjoy life in his dorm in Ashlin house, despite the sense of loneliness and of being abandoned by his family, his shyness and timidity, and the brace on his teeth. There was, of course, no lack of hurtful comments from his schoolmates. However, if nothing else, those years of loneliness at boarding school taught him resilience and self-reliance. No doubt music helped him through; his aunt had encouraged his parents to pay for piano lessons for him at the school, which they did, and Farrokh could play a song note perfect after just one hearing. And there was the school choir, which Farrokh joined together with many of his classmates.

But there were friends in boarding school, too, such as Subash Shah, also from Zanzibar, and four other boys with whom Farrokh would listen to the radio; pop music, rather than the Indian and classical music which filled the air around them. Elvis was king, though Farrokh also developed an eclectic taste for Cliff Richard, Little Richard and Fats Domino. He also morphed from Farrokh into Freddie, a name that his family would also adopt.

Freddie was able to develop his sense of the dramatic, which stood him in good stead in later years in his career, by joining the school's drama society, where he proved to be dramatically uninhibited, even "*frenzied*", according to one friend.

But it was music that was at the centre of the boys' attention, and within three years Freddie and his four friends, Derek Branch, Bruce Murray, Farang Irani and Victory Rana, had formed their own band, appropriately named The Hectics. The group gave Freddie his first taste of adoring fans when girls from the neighbouring school began screaming for the boys in white shirts and black ties, their hair greased back, when they played at school functions. Yet it was the good-looking Bruce who was the front man; at the time, Freddie was quite happy to remain behind him, singing accompanying vocals and playing the piano. (Even here, facts are hard to come by, friends' memories parting company about whether he was called Freddie, Farrokh, and even Buckwee, or Bucky, because of his protruding teeth. Similarly, no one can agree about whether there was a general awareness during his school years that he was gay, even though he had started to use the term "*Darling*" when talking to some of this friends. Boarding school was a confusing time for many boys, and in later years, Freddie would hint at the truth in rumours of homosexual affairs in school, but, as usual, would refuse to go any deeper into the details about his past.)

Brian May, in the meantime, had passed his Eleven-Plus exams and was now attending Hampton Grammar School, and his academic excellence continued, although by now he had teamed up with a fellow student called Dave Dilloway, who was also learning to play the guitar. And whenever they met in school it was music that they talked about even at the back of the classroom, which still didn't stop Brian from excelling academically. Like Freddie, he joined the school drama club, perhaps in an attempt to build his confidence, for he, too, was an insecure teenager.

Harold May proved an invaluable ally in Brian's musical life, helping him build an electric guitar from scratch — without a lathe, and using buttons and motorcycle springs — an instrument that accompanied Brian from then for on forty-five years, acquiring the name the 'Red Special'. Now also armed with a homemade bass guitar for Dave and two reel-to-reel tape recorders, Brian and Dave started experimenting with playback, whilst trying to get a band together. The lineup began to change almost as soon as it was fixed, eventually finding peace with Brian, Dave, John "*Jag*" Garnham on guitar, Richard Thompson on drums, John Sanger on piano and singer Tim Staffell. Together they formed a blues band known as '1984', taken from George Orwell's novel.

Brian confessed later to using his guitar as "*a shield to hide behind*", but although still shy and unsure of himself, he had acquired a girlfriend, Pat, although she never seemed to go to any of the band's gigs. Brian was a "*goody two shoes*" according to John Garnham, certainly not extrovert on or off the stage, and certainly gave no inkling that he would transform into the arm-swinging "*Great Rock Guitarist*" of Queen fame. Brian was Mr. "*Super-Brain*".

Roger Taylor's was no lazy brain, either, and at the age of 11, in 1960, he was granted a choral scholarship to Truro Cathedral School, but when his academic qualifications led to an offer for Truro school, that town's prestigious educational establishment, that is where he headed next. And that wasn't the only change in his life, because when a cousin introduced to him to the joys of Jerry Lee Lewis and Elvis Presley, the ukulele was history, the guitar was the new king in his bedroom. But not for long; Roger found himself attracted to his mother's saucepans upon which he

clattered with knitting needles. And not long after that, in 1961, a snare drum, a cymbal, a bass drum and a tom-tom could be found trembling beneath his enthusiastic hands.

By 1964 he could be found playing drums in a trio with two of his schoolmates on bass guitar and guitar in a band that they called The Cousin Jacks, or Beat Unlimited, when they were joined by a singer, the gigs at school functions and private parties began to materialise, and the third member of Queen had finally hit the stage.

Roger Taylor and his fellow band member Mike Dudley, however, had greater ambitions; one year later, they were both playing in a group called The Reactions with a local musician who glorified in the name of Johnny Quale, whose hero was Elvis. Roger proved to be more ambitious than any of them, constantly asserting that he was "*gonna be a pop star*"; and while The Reactions gigged around Cornwall through the summer, Taylor was dreaming to the sounds of The Who — whose lineup boasted Roger's drumming hero, Keith Moon — and the Yardbirds.

Before the year was out, Quale had left the band as a consequence of an argument and with their new singer, the band launched into rock or high-energy soul, with Roger singing lead vocals on occasion. They were even good enough to win the Rock and Rhythm Championship at Truro City Hall, and were thenceforth known as "*The Champion Group of Cornwall*". They were a good band, performing as the opening act for no lesser luminaries than The Kinks and Gerry and The Pacemakers, and their singing drummer was one of a kind. As, indeed, with his blonde good looks, was his attraction for the opposite sex; he was never short of girlfriends, shall we say.

As 1967 played out, The Reaction, as they were now called, were being influenced by the like of Cream and another artist who would help Roger to align with his future bandmates in Queen, Jimi Hendrix. Hendrix's drummer, Mitch Mitchell, became another of Roger's heroes.

The Reaction, even under Roger's eager guidance, had already begun to have internal problems and was about to stutter through its final year. 1967 was also the year that Roger left school in Truro having secured several O-levels and three A-levels, which he gained in Biology, Chemistry and Physics. Roger was off to London where he'd been offered a place at the London School of Medicine in Whitechapel to study for a dentistry degree. At his mother's behest, the drum kit stayed behind. Roger revived his band briefly in the summer of 1968, but when the autumn arrived and the musicians went their separate ways, The Reaction was no more. (Having become bored with dentistry, Roger changed to Biology and eventually obtained a BSc from the East London Polytechnic.)

Freddie's academic achievements, on the other hand, waned towards the end of his school life, and he left St Peter's without any O-levels. In his early years, Freddie had proven to be a good student, winning the Junior All-Rounder prize age of 12; he had shown himself to be a good sportsman in cricket and hockey. He displayed the steely determination, the "*I can do it*" attitude that was to bring him so far in his career, when he took up boxing, refusing to give up even with blood spurting from his mouth.

In 1962, school was over and Freddie returned home to Zanzibar. Never again would he return to St. Peter's, eager to move away from India and get on with his life.

Freddie's parents wanted him to continue his education, so back to school he went, in Stone Town this time, where he was reunited with Subush Shah, taken away from India because he had failed an exam.

Music was by now becoming increasingly important in Freddie's life, and both music and his life were being subjected to upheavals, because as the 60s arrived so did the end of colonial rule in Zanzibar, whilst in Britain, the Beatles were about to change the music scene forever.

The handover from colonial rule did not take place without violent

revolution, however, and in June 1964, Freddie's friend Shah and his family left Zanzibar for Ohio, USA, where a state scholarship awaited the young man — ironically, for a family hoping to escape violence, at Kent State University.

Freddie's family also fled the violence, Freddie later telling a friend that his father had been threatened with decapitation by the rebels, and as his father Bomi was a British citizen, the family chose England for their place of refuge, settling in the London suburb of Hounslow, where they bought a house and Freddie's parents found work. Freddie proved to be the rock of optimism the kept the family's spirits afloat; he was delighted to be in England however difficult circumstances might now be for them, despite the loss of the "*ivory-white piano*" and the comfortable life they had enjoyed, and Zanzibar was now as far away for him as the moon. But what was he to do?

His lack of qualifications was a hindrance, so in September 1964 he began a two-year course at Isleworth Polytechnic to get the A-level he needed to enter Ealing Technical College and School of Art.

Still shy, still sensitive, still lonely and still different from his fellow students because of his slightly gauche manner and fashion sense, Freddie, that nonetheless, made friends of those boys who valued his artistic nature. And that creativity was apparent from the moment he attended the Polytechnic, because he was soon playing, by ear, standing at an upright piano in the assembly hall, any popular songs that his schoolmates wanted to hear. His was a unique gift, as was his talent for improvising around the melodies. It was clear that music was becoming increasingly important in his life; he joined the school choir, and although unsure of himself, his friends noted that he could still be quite be an exhibitionist, and he was certainly thrilled with the attention. Two of those friends, Adrian Morrish and Patrick Connolly, would spend time at Fred's house; listening to music, of course. There was also music to be found at parties, dances, pubs and clubs, and Freddie was no slouch as far as his social life was concerned, soaking up all the musical influences that he could get his ears close to; he found the money by doing layouts for a magazine. Not that he was particularly good at the work, by all accounts, despite his desire to go to art college.

With Freddie now in the same country at least, the paths of the future rock band were gradually converging. Soon after Freddie's arrival at the Polytechnic, Brian was rejoicing in the first gig for his band,1984, at a youth club in Twickenham on the 28th of October 1964; another member of Queen was up and running.

The first to drop out of Brian's new band was John Sanger, who had accepted a place at Manchester University. Undaunted, the group continued to gig in school halls and youth clubs. But the passing months saw band members depart for far-flung universities, and when the autumn of 1965 arrived it was time for Brian to hang up his Hampton Grammar School hat as well, the proud possessor of 10 O-levels and four A-levels, which were in Physics, Pure Mathematics, Applied Mathematics and Additional Mathematics; for the academic whizz-kid, a three-year degree course in physics and infra-red astronomy beckoned at London's Imperial College of Science and Technology.

The new influences around Freddie at the polytechnic had begun their work in Freddie's mind; his clothing changed and he became more fashionable; he and Patrick Connolly, who turned out to be a guitarist, and a fellow student called Paul Martin joined forces to sing around Freddie's piano in their spare time.

But then, Isleworth Polytechnic also became an event in his past; it was September 1966, the year of 'Paint it Black' and '19th Nervous Breakdown' by the Rolling Stones, 'Paperback Writer' and 'Yellow Submarine' by the Beatles and 'Summer in the City' by the Loving Spoonful — and Freddie was about to head to Ealing College of Art with that precious A-level in his pocket.

But by the time he got there, Freddie was a changed young man, because he'd recently seen his undefined dream materialise in front of his eyes in the shape of guitarist Jimi Hendrix, who, at the time, was mesmerising London with his furious guitar playing. Freddie was awestruck; in Hendrix, he saw style, enormous stage presence, fierce talent and fearless clothing; Hendrix, in fact, was everything that Freddie aspired to become.

Brian's band,1984, soldiered on into that year of 1966 that filled Brian's ears with magical new sounds from the Yardbirds and Jeff Beck, Eric Clapton and Cream and, of course, the Jimi Hendrix Experience.

BRIAN AND FREDDIE HAD FINALLY TUNED IN TO THE SAME WAVELENGTH.

But for Brian, the end of his association with 1984 was approaching, despite his brush with greatness when the band appeared on the same bill as his hero Jimi Hendrix at the Olympia Theatre in 1967, on the 26th of July. The pressure on Brian from trying to play with the band and keep up with the demands of his difficult course proved overwhelming, and as the spring of 1968 rolled around, Brian yielded to the inevitable and left the band.

Freddie was now taking in the sights and sounds of the same art school that had harboured, Pete Townshend, Ron Wood, Eric Clapton, Keith Richards, Jimmy Page, and Charlie Watts. His first port of call, however, was the fashion design course, where, in between working as a baggage handler at Heathrow Airport at the weekends, watching budding musicians and going to the pub with his friends, his time was taken up with fabric printing, textile technology and pattern design. Within the year, however, he had decided to move over to the graphics department, or rather, the college principal had ejected him from the fashion course, ostensibly for taking too much time off to watch Jimi Hendrix play.

It was a fortuitous move, because the graphics course was also attending by Tim Staffell, 1984's lead vocalist, together with other students equally interested in music, so conversations moved over a range of musical topics taking in Jimi Hendrix and moving on through to classical composers. Hendrix was still Freddie's hero — Freddie once went to see him for 14 consecutive nights — and he never missed an opportunity to impersonate him, playing air guitar or a ruler, it didn't matter; he was obviously enthusiastic, but no one believed he would commit himself for long enough to make it in a band.

It wasn't long before Tim introduced his college friends to 1984, and Freddie, the "*curious sponge*" in his classmates' words, was immediately impressed with them.

Tim Staffell had, by now, also left 1984 behind him, and he, organist Chris Smith and Brian wanted to form a new group; but what they needed was a drummer. And they wanted a "*Ginger Baker/Mitch Mitchell*" clone, so read their advert on the Imperial College noticeboard, at any rate.

What they got was Roger Taylor — even though for his audition he had to play the bongos as his kit was still down in Cornwall. When he sang, the deal was clinched; Brian thought him the best drummer he'd ever seen, and the exuberant "*…excellent… really confident and flamboyant*", according to Tim Staffell, the good-looking, the optimistic and ambitious Taylor was on board.

There was no doubt that Tim Staffell thought up the name Smile for the group, but there was more doubt about their debut performance at Imperial College, where they supported either The Troggs or Pink Floyd, depending on who's telling the story. Whichever it was, Brian, standing out for the wrong reasons with his afro hairstyle and bri-nylon shirt, was a step closer to his dream of becoming a professional musician.

Nonetheless, academia still claimed them; Chris Smith and Tim Staffell had one more year at Ealing, although by now Roger had decided to leave his dentistry course, telling his mother he wanted to concentrate on music for just one year. Brian intended to stay

on at Imperial to work on a PhD, having been invited to engage in astronomical research at Jodrel Bank Observatory on the grounds that "*Brian was first and foremost a bright physicist*", in the words of one of his college professors, Sir Bernard Lovell. "*Everybody thought I was a bit of an eccentric for wanting to be out there looking at the stars*", Brian recalled years later, "*but I still do*".

Freddie was still living at home at the time, although spending a great many of his free hours at Chris Smith's flat and, for the time being, still only on the musical periphery. But that was all about to change very rapidly. Both Brian and Roger were ambitious, and when they played, they wanted to play better than anyone else, and it was soon clear that Chris was not going to survive. Smile were heading towards a heavy rock style, which is not where Chris Smith wanted to be; in February 1969, just before a gig at the Royal Albert Hall in London, Chris was asked to leave the group, although his memory of that time is that he told the band that he wasn't going to play for them any more.

So, organ-less, Smile went to the fundraiser concert at the Royal Albert Hall, where such illustrious names as Joe Cocker and the Bonzo Dog Doo-Dah Band were also appearing. They managed to complete their set, despite Tim accidentally unplugging his bass.

More gigs followed, down in Cornwall through Roger's connections, interspersed with a trip to London for a gig in April 1969, where Mercury Records boss Lou Reizner watched them play — and impressed by their harmonies and big riffs that reminded him of Led Zeppelin immediately offered them a deal to record a single for release in the US; a "*let's see what happens*" contract. The single consisted of two of Tim's songs, 'Earth', an appropriate choice, for Neil Armstrong would set a man's foot on the moon for the first time on the 21st of July, and 'Step on Me', the writing of songs being an ambition shared by both Tim and Brian.

There were now more gigs in the offing, because the group had signed to the Rondo Talent Agency in London, also home to

Genesis and Nick Drake. Smile opened for a variety of bands and John Garland, for one, thought that he detected the spark of greatness. So, it seemed, did a certain Freddie Bulsara, who often accompanied the band, his enthusiasm obvious from the number of ideas and suggestions for musical improvements that came bubbling out of him. Although he said nothing, it was becoming obvious that Freddie would have loved to be part of Smile. But Tim was the frontman and he had no intention of relinquishing that role.

Freddie, with his black hair now long and flowing, his rockstar-in-waiting androgynous style, silk scarves and satin and velvet clothing may have been shy, but he was not backward in coming forward about how to change the music for the better; especially the presentation and costumes — Smile wore jeans and T-shirts on stage. Freddie felt that the rock experience should be similar to going to watch a musical; a visual feast for the eyes as well as an audio feast for the ears.

Fired by his enthusiasm for Smile, Freddie was now saying publicly that he was going to be a pop star, which, of course, no one took very seriously as he wasn't even known as a singer, although everyone knew that he played piano in the college whenever he could, and often when he was supposed to be attending lectures.

It wasn't long before Freddie plucked up the courage to start singing with Tim, Chris and others to amuse their classmates; and even then, at that early stage, his voice made an impression on those who heard it. But he was anxious to go even further and start writing songs; in fact, he was passionate about writing songs according to Chris Smith. And it was to Chris that he turned for help to get songs together, and the two of them tried to construct a piece from the note scraps that Freddie would bring to their meetings. It didn't come as easily to him as he had hoped, and he was often in despair at his inability to write; he and Chris barely managed to get one song completed; 'The Cowboy Song', as Chris recalls, which against all the odds proved to be the midwife to one of Queen's most successful songs ever, 'Bohemian Rhapsody', as they both contain the immortal line, 'Mama I just killed a man'. And by all accounts, Freddie was ready to kill to become a mega star; he was certainly ready to burst with frustration. And the lunchtime concerts in the college that would see the talents of bands such as Tyrannosaurus Rex strut onto the stage, fired up Freddie even more, although the closest he got to stardom was to help carry their equipment.

SMILE WERE NO CLOSER, EITHER.

They did, however, at least have a record contract, and even though their first single had ended up on Skid Row, Mercury Records was considering an album. At least the band could get into a studio, which they did in September that year to cut an EP that, although it was graced with May's increasingly skilful guitar playing and Staffell's voice — which resembled a softer version of the future Queen front man's own soaring vocals — was shelved for almost fifteen years. "*Rough around the edges*", was how one man, Terry Yeadon, who worked at Pye Studios as a maintenance engineer, described the Smile that he heard one night in the Pye recording studios for a session that he had arranged — illegally. Yeadon harboured ambitions to be a producer, and the group had probably been brought to his attention by Christine Mullen, Brian's girlfriend. If nothing else, at least Smile would now have a professionally recorded audition tape to haul in front of the record companies.

RIGHT: Members of the group Smile posed in Addison Gardens, West Kensington, London in August 1969. Left to right: Bruce Sanderson (with eye patch), Paul Humbertone, Brian May (sitting on bonnet), Pete Edmunds, Tim Staffell, Clive Armitage and Paul Fielder

THE QUEEN'S COURTIERS

Freddie, who had departed from Ealing art college before taking his final exams, didn't know it, but the moment for his first, very modest, step up the ladder towards fame had arrived; along a convoluted route, it's true, but it came nonetheless. And once again, the connection was through Brian's girlfriend.

Christine was studying at the Maria Assumpta teacher training college in London, which was where Roger's girlfriend was also studying, as was a girl called Pat McConnell. An important link had been forged, because Pat knew them both and had seen Smile play. Pat was the older sister to Helen McConnell; and Helen McConnell was Ken Testi's girlfriend.

BUT WHO WAS KEN TESTI?

Ken Testi was the young, unofficial driver-cum-manager-cum-roadie for a Liverpudlian group calling themselves Ibex that had gone down to London for the summer months to see if fame might beckon them, too. One night, Pat and the Ibex boys went to meet Smile at the Kensington Tavern, before they all adjourned to Pat's flat. Freddie Bulsara went, too.

Inevitably, the Smile boys began to strut their stuff — and so did Freddie Bulsara, who knew all the lyrics to the songs and could even sing harmony. Freddie's desire to be a pop star had finally burst the damm to overcome his innate shyness, and he had become confident, even pushy. And if Ibex needed one thing, it was a singer. And if Freddie needed one thing, it was a band, even though, as Ken Testi admitted, Freddie was shining and immaculately turned out, whereas the lads from Ibex were "*rough and ready*". Freddie seemed to them rather like an exotic butterfly. No matter. Needs must when Freddie was driving was in charge.

The summer passed with the two groups spending their free time together moving between flats and listening to records of their favourite bands, Jimi Hendrix to the fore, until it was time for Ibex to honour to bookings at the Octagon Theatre in Bolton in the north of England on August the 23rd, followed by an open-air festival gig.

What the Ibex boys didn't know was that Freddie had never sung on stage before. But Freddie's new-found confidence wasn't going to let an insignificant fact like that stop him now. Shyness still plagued him, though, and he would often revert to it; once he had stopped 'acting' during a song, his announcements of the next song would be strangely polite and reserved. Offstage, however, he could be chatty and strike with biting witticisms.

The new Ibex lineup got stuck into 'Jailhouse Rock', if memory serves them right, and the original trio may have wondered why Freddie kept his back to the audience for the first half of the opening song. In fact, the ruse gave Freddie time to calm his jangled nerves, settle his voice and then turn to the audience with confidence restored. He could do it. He could sing. The final piece on the Queen chessboard was moving into place.

Importantly, Brian had managed to attend one of the concerts; so when the call that Freddie had longed for eventually came, only one person needed to answer. He wasn't quite there yet, though; he still had more of his apprenticeship to serve. Part of the reason for that was, Ibex was living on borrowed time. Once again, it was academia that did the damage. Guitarist Mike Birsin went off to Liverpool Art College in the autumn, and Ken Testi was considering leaving as well. And then one last gig for Ibex came up, also in Liverpool. So Freddie, Roger Taylor, Brian May and the rest of the gang, piled into the van and headed northwards, which 'Tupp' Taylor the bass player, remembers

RIGHT: Freddie Mercury during an interview with the Daily Express at his Shepherd's Bush flat, London, 1969

as delivering "*awful*" renditions of the likes of Led Zeppelin's 'Communication Breakdown' or Cream's 'We're Going Wrong'; Freddie's showmanship was fantastic, he added, but his pitching was off. When Brian and Roger Taylor joined in for an encore, the phantom lineup of Queen had played together for the first time.

Freddie's "*I want to be a pop star*" obsession was pushing him forward, and his next move, having gained the approval of the others, was to rename the band, giving it a more dangerous ambience; Ibex was dead, long live Wreckage. Which is what he had stencilled all over the band's gear, showing an astute awareness of marketing and a focused ambition. New band, new song list, including original compositions by Freddie and Mike, showing that they had progressed from Freddie's early days of despair. Now that he had input into a band, there was no holding him, and he insisted that their own songs needed key changes to keep them interesting. On the only surviving recording of Wreckage rehearsing, it's Freddie who is calling the shots, Freddie trying to keep them concentrated.

Before the band could make its debut at Ealing Art College, Mick Smith, the drummer, told them that he was leaving, which aggravated Freddie no end. Fortunately, Richard Thompson was still in their orbit and slipped into the drummer's seat; all's well that ends well. Well, apart from the fact that the gig was considered to be a decided disaster, despite Freddie's "*posing and strutting*" and a brand-new white suit for the occasion.

Tim Staffell disliked life Freddie's coy, aware, display of narcissism, Freddie was finding his feet and cared less and

---

RIGHT: Members of English group Ibex posed in Bolton, Lancashire on 23rd August 1969. Left to right: Paul 'Flogger' Fielder, Unknown, Mike Bersin, Sian Ollett, Ken Testi, Helen McConnell, 'Miffer' Smith, 'Little Peggy', Richard Thompson, Freddie Mercury, Bruce Sanderson, Pat McConnell, Roadie Geoff Higgins (crouching) and John 'Tupp' Taylor

less, though unwilling to present himself as openly gay; in fact, one of his girlfriends maintained that, despite his attraction, he was also frightened about his sexual orientation. To most people at the time, apparently, he seemed heterosexual. It was hard to pigeonhole him; he was surrounded by good-looking girls, who were his platonic friends, and even had a relationship with a "*redheaded bombshell called Rosemary*" to whom, in her own words many years later, he was "*terribly attentive and brotherly*". It took two years before they became lovers; it was Rosemary who finally ended the relationship with her "*androgynous*" boyfriend.

Wreckage lived up to its name, driven into the buffers by lack of real ambition — except on Freddie's part — and survived for another few handfuls of gigs, the last being at Richmond Rugby Club as Christmas 1969 approached. For Freddie, it was time to reorganise his thoughts and find out how to overcome this hitch in his plans. He also needed to find a way to earn a living; but he had, at least, moved out of his parents' home and escaped their permanent state of horror at his proposed lifestyle. There was a stall in Kensington market selling, according to Ken, "*bits of tat really*", Edwardian and Victorian secondhand clothes amongst other things, which Freddie ran together with Roger Taylor; now and again there were drawing assignments as well as a period in Harrods in Knightsbridge.

More than anything, though, Freddie was anxious to get back in front of a band. To that end, he started searching the music press, coming up trumps when he discovered a band called Sour Milk Sea were looking for a vocalist. Even better, the band were professional and had opened for the likes of Deep Purple.

He attended the audition, his long dark hair flowing, bursting with confidence and "*dripping in velvet*", as founder member and guitarist Chris Chesney remembered, who was impressed by Freddie's falsetto singing, even if his voice was not the powerful instrument that it would later become. Once he'd auditioned, there was, of course, no one but Freddie for the job; he was "*Fantastic*" according to Chesney. Freddie debuted at Highfield Parish hall in Headington, Oxford in March 1970, and it wasn't long before he felt confident enough to start using his own lyrics in place of those the band had already written, also introducing dramatic chord changes; his interventions changed Sour Milk Sea's musical direction and Freddie's flamboyance rubbed off on Chris, too, releasing him to be more of a showman, although no one could compete with Freddie's swirling microphone stand and strutting vanity shot through with a good dose of humour.

Six years younger than Freddie, Chesney was quite happy to accommodate his new singer, and they started to collaborate on new songs. Between them, Chris and Freddie sparked new life into what was already quite a successful band in its small pool, and they became good friends, but Freddie was always reluctant to talk about his past. Chris even moved into Fred's house in West London, where he was able to jam with Brian May. Who, Chesney thought at the time, had not the slightest intention of using the quirky butterfly that was Freddie as the Smile front man.

Unfortunately, Freddie's larger-than-life character caused a small earthquake of discontented jealousy in Sour Milk Sea, which had turned into a serious problem within the space of a few weeks. The band split into two camps, Freddie and Chris facing off against Paul Milne the bassist and rhythm guitarist Jeremy Gallop. The latter considered that Freddie was watering down their underground, heavy blues sound in favour of massive commercial pop harmonies. The split left Paul, whose father was bankrolling the band, in tears. The disputes turned physical, and by the spring of 1970 Sour Milk Sea had ceased to exist after Paul had disbanded it and taken all of the equipment, which belonged to him.

ONCE AGAIN, FREDDIE WAS A MUSICAL
ORPHAN; AND ONCE AGAIN LADY LUCK
TOOK HIM UNDER HER WING.

Smile had been struggling to progress; Brian May was
heavily involved in science projects, but it was Tim Staffell
who finally put the knife in when he decided to call it a day.
His musical tastes had changed, and he was disillusioned
with the lack of success. Freddie anxiously persuaded May
and Taylor not to disband, and his persistence paid off.

FINALLY, FREDDIE WAS IN THE BAND THAT
HE HAD CONSIDERED HOME FROM THE
FIRST MOMENT HE HAD SEEN THEM PLAY.

This new and exciting moment in his life he celebrated by
changing his name to Freddie Mercury, inspired by a line
in a song he had written called 'My Fairy King', "*Oh mother
Mercury what have you done to me*".

The band's name changed, too, and Freddie's suggestion
that it should be called Queen, was accepted by the others.
It was, said Freddie, exactly the right name for his intended
tactics of shock and awe, "*Very regal, strong, universal,
immediate. Certainly I was aware of the gay connotations.
But it sounds splendid!*" enthused Freddie about the name.

Now, there was just one more piece of jigsaw puzzle to slip
into place, but before that could happen there were a few
hiccups to overcome — though not of Freddie's making
this time. Without Tim, there was no bass player; the first
new recruit in a short series of players was Mike Grose.
Who soon found the others' student lifestyles dispiriting,
used as he was to being busy working during the day and
playing gigs at night. Just a few months later he left… to be
replaced by Barry Mitchell, very slightly nonplussed by the
band's wrangles over details, not to mention Freddie's painful
attention to his hair and couture such as his tight one-piece

outfit. Neither, during his occupation of the bass player spot,
did he think that Freddie's voice was quite up to scratch; in
fact, he conceded later, "*there wasn't a lot of depth there*".
But Mitchell quelled any doubts he may have had because,
after all, the band was getting gigs, although they couldn't
live from the money as the fees were swallowed in expenses.
The market stall was dying on its legs, so it helped that a
man named Alan Mair, who owned the clothes stall across
the way from Freddie's, asked Freddie to look after his stall
from time to time.

Barry Mitchell wasn't long for the world of Queen, either, and
after a few gigs, Kensington's College of Estate Management
or the Cavern Liverpool, the new year of 1971 rolled around,
and January brought with it a support spot at the Marquee in
London. But by that time, Mitchell had taken the decision to
leave. Queen's musical direction, what he described as Led
Zeppelin meets Yes, was not his, and he felt that he was still
an outsider for the May, Taylor and Mercury triangle. Despite
Freddie's girlfriend, Mary Austin — Brian May's erstwhile
girlfriend, with whom Freddie eventually shared a flat, and
who grew to have complete trust in Freddie's kindness
towards her as he did in hers — trying to change his mind,
Mitchell's last gig arrived on the 9th of January 1971. The
gap behind Freddie opened up once again.

Matters seemed to go from bad to worse when Doug
Ewood was engaged and picked up the bass to plug the
gap. Although he thought he was doing well, unfortunately,
Doug had misread the road signs, and at his first gig on the
19th of February in Hornsey, London, the bassist began
leaping around; a bad decision to make behind Freddie's
ego. Afterwards, a displeased singer feigned distraught
depression at God and the world and Queen, of the "*I can't
go on*" variety, a display which the other two permanent
Queen members interpreted correctly, and just one gig later,
Douglas was no more.

The gap, however, still was. Except that now the musical muses had grown weary of their sport; the gap was about to be filled as a hand does a glove.

Shy, but known for keeping his cool in tight situations, John Deacon's personal characteristics would stand him, and his future band, in good stead.

In 1971, Queen were still without a bass player and began holding auditions in the Imperial lecture theatre to try and remedy the situation once and for all. Deacon, who had unsuccessfully been toying with the idea of getting back into playing his bass, decided to attend and launched into a blues jam. But it was when he joined in on three Queen songs that, as Brian May put it, "*We knew it was right*". Deacon had been on the beat throughout his audition, and his more measured, less heavy bass playing had won the day. As, indeed had the young man's reserved nature, which, the others felt, would act as a counterweight to their own histrionics.

QUEEN HAD THEIR FINAL COURTIER.

John Deacon slotted into that gap behind Freddie for the first time on July the 2nd 1971. He concentrated on his job, he didn't, nor had any desire to, distract from Freddie. John had a foretaste of what life might be like with this colourful crowd when they were all chased out of town in Cornwall where they had travelled for a gig.

Nonetheless, the hard reality was that Queen was still making no headway in the music world. Taylor became a student studying biology at North London Polytechnic, and Freddie closed the stall but continued to work for Alan Mair. It was dispiriting and Brian, whose insistence that the band had to be a finished product when their break finally arrived proved to be correct, was despairing, and his despair caused him to phone up an old acquaintance, Terry Yeadon, who

at that moment was wondering which band he could find to come and test out the acoustics in the new studio facility in North London in which he worked. Queen it would be, happy to be prodded on the petri dish in return for a professionally made studio demo of their music.

The sessions went on for a week and tested the group's patience severely as they were forced to stop and start and heave their equipment around all the studios. It was all worth it in the end, however, because when it was all over they had two-inch, sixteen-track masters containing five of their original songs; 'Liar', 'The Light Comes Down', 'Jesus', 'Keep Yourself Alive', and 'Great King Rat'.

More importantly, perhaps, John Anthony, who had produced Smile, had now formed his own company, Neptune Productions, together with the owners of Trident Studios. One of his two partners had gone to watch the Queen Sessions and liked what he heard, especially what he saw as a potential hit, 'Keep Yourself Alive'.

The demo did eventually serve its purpose, because although most companies that Ken Testi — now back on board and trying to make his way in the music business — were not interested and EMI and Decker didn't take the bait after Kent had managed to get appointments to see them, one company, B&C, which was part of Charisma Records, were interested. They even went so far as to offer £25,000 pounds coupled with a tour of Belgium to the group — who went away and thought about it and then rejected the offer, not wanting to dangle along at the bottom of the Charisma Christmas tree when Genesis was at the top. Which was very brave and sensible of them.

When Roger had a conversation with John Anthony about the Charisma offer, John and the band arranged to get together, and John Anthony told them that he would give them a better deal than the one offered by Charisma.

Norman Sheffield and his brother Barry were tough men, not people to mess around with, as producer Tony Visconti remembered, describing them as being "*like something out of the wild west*". They were the owners of Trident Studios — one of the best studios in the world, where likes of David Bowie, George Harrison and Elton John would go to record — and had also set up Trident Audio Productions, which would sign up bands. Norman had been urged by John Anthony not to miss the opportunity to sign Queen. So, in March 1972, Barry and John went down to Forest Hill in South London to see the band play.

This sudden interest in the group from different sides, seemed to herald the beginning of a breakthrough. And after the performance that included songs like 'Keep Yourself Alive' and 'See What a Fool I've Been', and one that especially impressed Barry, 'Big Spender', known from Shirley Bassey's version, Barry couldn't wait to get the band on board.

So Queen and the Sheffield brothers began discussions on a management deal under the aegis of Neptune Productions, which would give them access to the top-of-the-line, hi-tech Trident recording studios to record new material. In the meantime, Neptune would try and find a record label to sign the group. It was an extremely tempting offer but Queen took their time before accepting, going over the contracts carefully, and working on perfecting their sound on the advice of John Anthony, so that they could reorient towards playing in larger venues. It was time to get serious.

But by the time the next gig had arrived eight months later, the excitement of the early part of the year had subsided. Ken Testi was no longer part of the management, of course, since Trident had arrived on the scene. Queen had wanted him to stay on as their personal manager, but Ken's personal commitments back

in St. Helen's led him to reluctantly turn down the offer, one that he had been working towards for so long.

Even before contracts had been signed, the Norman brothers offered the group access to the Trident Studios to cut an album to present to record companies. But because the studio was so popular, the only spaces available were between eleven at night and two in the morning.

Unperturbed, aware of the enormous opportunity they had been offered and with John Anthony agreeing to produce the album, the band were ready, and Freddie proved that he had done his homework; he presented Anthony with a copy of Harpers and Queen informing him that he wanted sound that reflected the pictures in the magazine, all different in content and style. Opportunity had knocked and Freddie was ready to embrace it with open arms.

It wasn't the easiest way to record an album, stop and go in the middle of the night, and as John Anthony was also involved in other projects, recording with Queen in the early hours deprived him of sleep, until one night he simply collapsed on the studio floor from exhaustion and mononucleosis. He left for Greece to recover.

His replacement was Roy Thomas Baker, who had already engineered for well-known bands such as T-Rex. Baker was assisted now and again by Ken Scott, who had been at Abbey Road Studios and was also Bowie's co-producer and engineer. Bowie was recording at the same time as Queen. Illustrious company for the unknown band. Ken enjoyed the sessions and would recall that the band were right on the ball, and Freddie as outrageous as ever with his infectious camp manners, and his affectionate "*Dearie*" was adopted throughout studio.

They might have been unknown, but they weren't going to be

trodden underfoot, and just as they did amongst themselves, they argued in the studio about how instruments should be miked and the placement of the drums. The opposite, in fact, of how the Trident engineers wanted things done. As a result, "*big battles*" ensued with Roy Baker, who would hide behind technical explanations to get his way. Some songs would not make it to the final album, and May would tussle with Baker endlessly for the perfection they both wanted; but Baker was also responsible for producing the beautiful sound that Brian wanted from his guitar, far removed from the crashing chords preferred by many guitarists. Perhaps the band's confidence was rising rapidly thanks to remarks such as the one by Roy Baker when he told the band, "*I think you're going to be so famous soon you're not going to want to talk to me*".

When John Anthony returned, he wasn't happy with the final mix, so he, Freddie and Brian started rerecording and mixing. The smoothest working relationship the three of them developed produced an association that would survive for another six years and five more albums by Queen. Between them, they had produced the template sound for which Queen would be known, the vocal acrobatics, lush vocal harmonies and vast production values. Finally, the album, which they called simply, Queen, with five tracks by Freddie Mercury, four by Brian May and one by Roger Taylor, was ready to go out into the world. The Record buying public were treated to such delights as, 'Keep Yourself Alive', 'My Fairy King', Modern Times Rock 'n' Roll' and a voice from the past, 'Doing All Right', written by Tim Staffell together with Brian.

By the time September 1972 came around Queen had not been on stage for months and were still without a manager. Roger Taylor had graduated in biology, and Deacon had also graduated, though he would stay at college studying for an MSc. Brian was juggling several hats, teaching full-time, playing with Queen and writing his thesis. It was too much,

and Brian resigned from his teaching post at Stockwell Manor, where he had been teaching secondary school maths and science, a job which he had enjoyed, even though he found it a challenge to keep the students' attention. Brian was going through a difficult period; having completed his PhD, he was advised by his supervisor to keep working at it for a couple of months. When he brought it back, it still didn't satisfy, and at that point Brian began to think that if he didn't finally give up his studies and devote himself to the band, "*I'll end up regretting it*".

The Sheffield brothers now came up with an offer of £20 pounds for each band member per week. The offer did not extend to a sound engineer; he would have to be paid out of their wages.

It was time to start taking Queen's album out to the record companies, a task that John Anthony found was fraught with frustration; interest was less than enthusiastic, especially when a price of £30,000 pounds was mentioned for costumes and lighting set ups. To help matters along, the Sheffield brothers had engaged the service of Jack Nelson, to be a business manager and secure a record deal. Nelson soon morphed into the band's manager.

There was some good news though; a company called B. Feldman & Co. had arranged to handle Queen's publishing, which was a shot in the arm as the company was responsible for Deep Purple as well. The company would soon be taken over by EMI Music Publishing, a very propitious event for Queen.

With no record company deal and no other offers on the horizon, Queen finally signed the contracts with Trident on the 1st of November 1972. It was a risk for Trident, for although Freddie would always say, "*There was never any doubt, darling, never*" about Queen's success, no one else was quite so certain. And the fears seemed justified when, having arranged a showcase for the band in the Kings Road, Nelson's best efforts brought not one person from the A&R department of any record company to sit in the audience. But Nelson was persistent, and his efforts were producing results; CBS were now interested, and negotiations had gone so far as three re-drafts of a contract with Queen. And when the tape landed on the desk of Elektra Records' managing director Jack Holzman, Queen had again acquired another groupie. Holzman described the music as *"like a perfectly cut diamond"*, completely rounded, and he was astonished by it. Holzman was desperate to sign the band, and Nelson doubted that CBS were really on-board with what they called a country band, albeit *"one of the best"*.

The wheels were finally beginning to turn, and they gathered speed when 1973 arrived and Queen turned up at Langham 1 Studio belonging to the BBC in London's West End. There, they recorded vocals for four of the group's songs that were to be broadcast on Sounds of the Seventies, a radio program hosted by DJ John Peel. Queen had at last reached a wider audience and come to the attention of the pop music aficionados.

BUT THERE WAS BETTER STILL YET TO COME.

Roy Featherstone was the A&R executive at EMI, who were investing in a new record label, EMI Records. Queen's publisher, Ronnie Beck, met up with Featherstone at a music business conference in the south of France and foisted the Queen tape upon him; Featherstone was mesmerised and sent a telegram to say the band should talk to him before they did anything else, because *"I want this band on my record label"*.

In the ensuing negotiations, Trident rejected the initial offer from EMI, and their persistence paid off. After a revised

RIGHT: Queen rehearsing for their first major tour, 1973

RIGHT: Freddie Mercury rehearsing for their first major tour, 1973

offer, Queen signed on the dotted line with EMI in March 1973. They were on their way. And Jack Holzman was still extremely interested. Suddenly, it seemed that everyone wanted this new sound from a group that had no weak links and a wiz-kid guitarist in Brian May.

Disappointingly, therefore, their debut single with EMI, "*Keep Yourself Alive*', failed to chart, despite the New Musical Express falling over itself with enthusiasm, intoning that the band "*could be huge*".

Finally, the album could be released, and with Freddie in one of his characteristically magnificent poses on the front cover (intended to resemble the figurehead on the prow of an old sailing ship), it hit the streets on the 13th of July 1973.

It fared better than the single, at least, though again disappointingly could only reach number 32 in the UK charts. There were some positive reviews, however, amongst those less kind; Rolling Stone claimed that Queen had all the tools they needed to take over "*Zep's abdicated heavy metal throne*" and "*become a truly influential force in the rock world. Their debut album is superb*". AllMusic commented in later years that it had been "*a patchy but promising debut from a classic rock group*". And although the opener 'Keep Yourself Alive', failed to strike home at the time, in 2008, Rolling Stone ranked it 31st in the "*100 Greatest Guitar Songs of All Time*".

Still, amongst a welter of androgynous-looking pop heroes like David Bowie and Roxy music, Queen's debut album had not been musically coherent enough to make them stand out, and they worried that they might have missed the bandwagon. Freddie was, perhaps, more desperate than the others, wondering what the future held for him if the band didn't make it. To help make sure it did, he gave his all in a video the band made later in the year, in which his lithe figure and fluid voice can be seen in top form.

But with the records struggling, the support work in the wings had to continue unabated, and Trident engaged the services of Tony Brainsby as a publicist. Brainsby was big-time, with stars such as Paul McCartney and Cat Stevens on his books. It helped that Brainsby found Freddie's secrecy about his past and over-the-top camp character fascinating, because it would it be no easy task to convince the mighty and self-righteous music press that the "*posing ponces*" were even playing their own instruments. Even aspiring writers like Steve Rosen mistakenly showed no interest in the band, and fellow musicians like Paul Thompson from Roxy Music called them "*too contrived*".

Brainsby set to work to spread the Queen message in the teen magazines; the boys were highly educated — good for parents — their clothes were striking and unconventional and they had a magical guitarist.

But without product, the publicity would count for nought, and Queen themselves were more than anxious to get back into the studio for their second album. But this time they were determined that they would not play second string to any other groups as far as studio time was concerned. They were granted their wish; recording sessions would take place during the day.

TIME FOR A SECOND BITE AT THE CHERRY.

RIGHT: Queen rehearsing for their first major tour, 1973

Freddie had already worked out which direction he wanted the second album to take, and once again as a guide, he presented his bandmates with a visual feast, this time in a painting by Victorian artist Richard Dad, The Fairy Feller's Masterstroke, painted whilst he was incarcerated in Bethlehem Royal Hospital after murdering his father. In the painting, fantastical creatures inhabit a complex woodland landscape. By the time the band hit Trident's sixteen-track studio, the stream of ideas had turned into a waterfall.

The band went to town in an attempt to "*Break the boundaries*" in Taylor's words, letting loose with six part harmonies, layered vocals and sumptuous 'orchestral-sounding guitar' from Brian May; the recording took one month. It wasn't a concept album, but a general thread ran through a collection of songs. One side of the LP was called Side White and the other Side Black, with the band dressed in either black or white on the cover to correspond with the record inside.

Now it was time for Queen to get back into the live gigs, as they had hardly played on stage since early in the year, and they were due to support one of the hot bands of the moment, Mott the Hoople, on their upcoming tour, an honour for which EMI had paid.

Queen played at the Golders Green Hippodrome for the BBC, where they sang most of the songs from the new album and which they followed up with a trip to Germany and Luxembourg for some promotional dates. Two dates at Imperial College in November followed, and they were also looking for a sensational promotional photo from photographer Mick Rock, who had been invited to one of the concerts. He came up with the idea that the band should appear naked to the waist. The ruse worked, and like it or love it, it brought in the publicity they craved and needed. And if their already striking self-confidence needed boosting, a shot in the arm came from the three

encores from the full house at their Imperial College gig.

Rehearsals for the tour started in Fulham in London, and the Mott the Hoople musicians, wrapped in their winter woollens, were intrigued that in the freezing converted cinema, Freddie Mercury, Brian — who preferred a sixpenny piece to a plectrum — and their mates made no concessions to the cold with their costumes even for a rehearsal. The other thing that struck the Hoople boys was the enormous amount of energy that Queen invested in their shows on tour; they were "*trying too hard*" too "*frantic*", according to Morgan Fisher, pianist for the Hoople, which they didn't need to, because it seemed obvious they had what it took to get to the top.

But the two bands got on very well, even though they spent a lot of time together and travelled in the same coach on the tour. The camaraderie between musicians helped Queen through the difficult gigs, when diehard Hoople fans rebelled against the camp support act and on one infamous occasion even resorted to throwing a very accurately aimed hotdog at Freddie. But the marksman was on the wrong side of history, for this was Mott's swan song, and by December, frontman Ian Hunter would have left the group.

The tour moved onto London for two final performances and the biggest audience that the Queen men had ever seen, some seven thousand people, and as the tour came to an end, the Queen boys were absolutely certain that they were the stars of the future, which made their frustration all the greater that their single and album were performing so poorly. And there were still months before Queen II would be released, thanks to the British government's three-day week, which had restricted electricity supplies, and before the start of another tour.

So, 1974 had the potential to be a cracking year for the band; but it started very inauspiciously in January in Australia with a fight between the stage crews for Queen and Aussie pub

RIGHT: Queen posed in lead singer Freddie Mercury's flat, Holland Road, West Kensington, London in early 1974

"WIMPOID ROYALOID HEAVYOID ANDROID VOID"

Madder Lake. No matter; they knew that they were on the rise when they were voted the second Most Promising Newcomers by the New Musical Express readers. Little by little they were making headway, and another boost came in February when they were invited onto BBC TV's Top of the Pops.

Two problems arose; Freddie balked at having to mime to playback, and the next single, 'Seven Seas of Rhye' wasn't ready for release. Freddie's misgivings were overcome, however, and in the light of the BBC invitation, Trident put their skates under the 'Seven Seas of Rhye', which entered the BBC charts at number 45.

The new tour began on the 3rd of March 1974, and would see Freddie Mercury playing the piano on stage for the first time in "*White Queen*", "*Seven Seas Of Rhye*" and "*The Fairy Feller's Masterstroke*". But on the second date, Brian felt a pain in his arm. It seems that the injections administered to the band for their Australia trip hadn't been completely sterile; Brian's arm became swollen, and he was found to have contracted gangrene. The infection would take its toll in the weeks to come.

Finally, on the 8th of March, Queen II was released. It contained "*The March of the Black Queen*", which Freddie Mercury had composed on the piano in 1973. Mercury's vocals cover two and a half octaves. Many fans consider this a precursor to Bohemian Rhapsody as it is written with two different time signatures simultaneously, 8/8 and 12/8 and includes a simpler polyrhythm in the uptempo section at the end, a rarity in popular music, and the song was so complicated the band couldn't play it live in its entirety.

And there was the "*biggest stereo experiment*" Queen had ever made, when they used panning in the mix of "*The Fairy Feller's Masterstroke*"; the music did credit to the intense painting of the same name.

Queen II did not fare too well out in the wider world: "*The dregs of Glam rock. Weak and overproduced*"; "*Wimpoid royaloid heavyoid android void*"; "*There is no depth of sound or feeling*"; or perhaps best — or worst — of all, the Winnipeg Free Press lambasted Queen II as an "*over-produced monstrosity*". But it was too late for the press to halt them in their tracks; the Queen bandwagon was on the move, and the album went to number five in the UK with the single "*Seven Seas Of Rhye*" getting to number 10 in the UK; the band had their first chart hit.

As the tour moved from venue to venue — some of which, in the light of the increasing success of the album and single, seemed ridiculously small-scale — the band's image, and Freddie's image of himself, crystallised, with Freddie's onstage persona becoming evermore outlandish, more obviously gay. But whenever problems arose technically or in the band relationships, it was often Mercury who would remain upbeat, despite his continuing tendency to indulge in his "*woe is me*" complaints. Yet Mercury was suffering in another way; from nerves that would cause him to throw up before a show. Freddie would need to remain upbeat, because already the rock music ambience was catching up with them, complete with injured fans and road crew and flashing blue police lights.

And those nerves were in evidence backstage on the night when Queen were the headline act for their biggest audience to date in the 3,500-seat Rainbow Theatre in London at the end of March. John Anthony had to both encourage and try to calm the singer, who swept onto the stage in a Zandra Rhodes creation; a white-winged costume that kept every eye upon him as he strode from musician to musician.

There was hardly time to draw breath before the band appeared in Denver, USA, to start another tour with Mott the Hoople; an odd experience, as they were once again back in the role of support act.

Nonetheless, America would be a puzzling and extraordinary experience; they were a band living on next to nothing, sharing hotel rooms, initially unknown to the wider American public, and the audience responses lacked the enthusiasm of the UK fans. And Queen noticed that they were attracting fans from amongst those on the periphery of society.

For Brian though, the American tour had unexpected consequences; he fell in love with a girl, identified only as 'Peaches', in New Orleans, a city that would retain Brian's affections from then on. And there was something less pleasant in store for Brian, too. The rockstar life, the drinking, the bad food and late nights coupled with the infection in his arm had produced a bout of jaundice. Brian had woken up one morning to find himself almost immobile; the diagnosis was hepatitis. Mercury too, had come out in boils. It was evident that they could not continue the tour, and bitterly disappointed that their tour was over, they flew back to England, where May was told to rest for six weeks in bed. It was unfortunate timing, as they were unable to capitalise on the release of 'Seven Seas of Rhye' in the US, which failed to chart as a result.

WHILST BRIAN WAS RECOVERING IN HOSPITAL, THE OTHER MEMBERS OF THE BAND BEGAN TO WORK ON SONGS FOR A THIRD ALBUM.

Eager to get going, Brian joined them, but it was too soon, and in August he collapsed and was taken to King's Hospital, where tests discovered a duodenal ulcer. It required an operation and, yet again, bed rest. Everyone was nervous about Brian's illness, none more so than Brian himself, who feared he might be replaced. "*I can't even get out of bed to participate in this*", he worried. "*Maybe the group will have to go on without me.*"

By the time Brian returned, there was an immense amount of work to catch up on. He was definitely not fully recovered from his illness, and yet the boys were working 14 or 15 hour days in the studio giving it their all. It was gruelling work. They had decided to make their songs clearer, less layered, because Queen II had confused people. This time they wanted hits, and Freddie had come up with 'Killer Queen', written in one night; it took a lot longer to get the backing vocals right. Brian was soon back in the swing with four songs of his own, songs that would become cornerstones in the Queen pantheon such as 'Now I'm Here', which he wrote whilst still in hospital and which was recorded in the final studio week, and 'Brighton Rock'.

By the end of September, the recording sessions were over. Queen II had reached 100,000 sales, and the single 'Killer Queen' was released in October. Brian was nervous that it wasn't powerful enough, and they were desperate for a big hit after the mishaps of the recent past. 'Killer Queen' surpassed his and everyone's expectations and rocketed to number 2 in the UK charts. It made the charts in six other countries, too, and came in at number 12 in the US, their first international hit. "*Killer Queen' was the turning point,* " Brian commented later. "*It was the song that best summed up our kind of music.*"

On the Sheer Heart Attack album, everyone got in on the act, even John Deacon for the first time individually with a gentle pop piece entitled 'Misfire', and Roger Taylor produced one of his best songs to date, 'Tenement Funster'. Freddie contributed five and collaborated with the others on a sixth, 'Stone Cold Crazy'. The ballad 'Lily of the Valley', although no one outside of the band could have known it, displayed Freddie's torn personality and pain at the time. It was, said Brian May many years later, about Freddie "*looking at his girlfriend and realising that his body needed to be somewhere else*".

The Band had wanted to experiment, not to be afraid, and Freddie's extraordinary voice, the production values and the songs did just that to brilliant effect. "*We took it to extreme, I suppose, but we are very interested in studio techniques and wanted to use what was available*", Freddie commented.

LEFT: Queen posing with actress and Queen Elizabeth II look-alike, Jeannette Charles, September 1974

"Wimpoid Royaloid Heavyoid Android Void"

"*The true unveiling of Queen... the moment where they truly came into their own*", was the AllMusic review later in the wake of a welter of excellent reviews. "*A feast. No duffers*" was the MNE's opinion, whilst The Winnipeg Free Press read, "*Brian May's multi-tracked guitar, Freddie Mercury's stunning vocalising and Roy Thomas Baker's dynamic production work*", presented a "*full-scale attack on the senses*". Sheer Heart Attack was ranked third best album of the year by Disc. The band could be well pleased with themselves. They might still be a cult band, but that, too, would vanish, just as Freddie's past seemed to have.

Whilst success was still coyly approaching them, and although their glamorous stage performances and sold-out performances suggested otherwise, the four boys had no money to lead a full-blown rock 'n' roll lifestyle — although Freddie and Roger dived headfirst into it when they got the chance. Brian was far less keen to do so. Freddie was still living with his girlfriend, and Taylor was still in his bed sit as was John Deacon, who was soon to marry Veronica Tatzlaff, his girlfriend of over 3 years, who was expecting their first child. Brian May was living in one room in Earls Court, which he could only get into through the boiler room. "*We had*", he said many years later, "*a single gas ring and no water*". Something needed to change, and the thing that needed to change was Trident, whose association with the band had become fraught. Lawyers were brought in to try and invalidate the contracts.

Meanwhile, 'Now I'm Here', one of Brian May's songs that had first been performed on the Sheer Heart Attack Tour in Manchester on the 30th of October 1974, was released as a single on the 17th of January 1975. It would climb to a very respectable number 11 in the UK charts.

In that new year of 1975, it was time to get back to the USA — where Sheer Heart Attack would work it's way up to number 12 in the charts — and try to win over audiences there after the truncated tour of the year before. Armed with the warning that mid-west audiences might balk at the name Queen, they set off for rehearsals in New York before their first date on the 5th of February 1975 in Columbus, Ohio; they would follow America with Japan and then Europe later in the year.

It seemed like there might be a repeat of the previous year's cancellation, this time because of concerns about Freddie, who began to experience vocal problems; three weeks into the tour, he was beginning to lose his voice with a possible case of nodules on his vocal cords. He had, in fact, strained his voice and had laryngitis. Six shows had to be cancelled after Mercury experienced severe pain following the Washington gig, and painkillers had to be administered to him.

By March the 8th in Chicago, he was back to his overweening self, a character that some would always find hard to take if not obnoxious. The voice problems returned, however, and the final date had to be cancelled, after which the band headed home and then off to Hawaii for a warm break before launching into the Japan leg of the tour for another eight concerts.

When they reached Japan, all memories of past difficulties were practically erased when the Japanese fans put on a display of excited enthusiasm. There were sold-out concerts of 14,200-seat venues with the noise the fans made deafening and the stage filling up with presents thrown to the boys. All of a sudden, the Queen musicians were superstars, "*overwhelmed*", in Brian May's words. It was just the fillip they needed. Even though they were quickly brought back down to earth when they went home to London and near penury (Brian had fungus growing on his bathroom walls) a state at which Freddie, particularly — now the proud recipient of an Ivor Novello Award for 'Killer Queen' — was getting very angry. The drawbacks of having your record company as your management were becoming all too evident. Brian was offered a job by an American rock group, and elated by their treatment

in Japan with which Queen could now compare their lifestyle in the UK, the resentment and frustration very soon came to a head. A confrontation with Trident was inevitable, and when it came, the band learned that they were actually in debt to the Sheffield Brothers, who had, to be fair, invested well over £200,000 in the group. Yet, as so often in the creative industry, the musicians were at the bottom of the pile when it came to who would be remunerated first.

The group took matters into their own hands and started looking for a new manager. They were wary of signing with someone who had a roster of big stars already, but in the end they signed with a man called John Reid, despite the fact that Elton John was on his books. Reid would represent Elton John for the next 28 years, and he would stay with Queen for the next three.

A deal was negotiated with Trident, and Queen Publishing now passed to EMI Publishing; their record deals would also no longer be the province of Trident, and the Sheffield Brothers would receive £100,000 in "*severance fees*" and 1% of the royalties for the next six Queen albums. The hurt at their treatment at the hands of Trident had been deep and would prove to be long-lasting. But, at last, there was hope that they could finally move forward free of the Sheffield Brother's shackles.

It was August 1975, the month that Queen had signed the agreement with Trident, and with fresh hope they headed to Herefordshire for rehearsals for their new album. They would call it A Night at the Opera; little did they know that it was destined to propel them dramatically out of the life they had known until then. Of the twelve tracks on the album cover, it was track number eleven that was destined to put the name of Queen in front of the eyes of the world. And it was Freddie Mercury who struck gold.

By now, the band had a tried and trusted method of working, whereby each would work up his own songs and then present

LEFT: Queen at the Tokyo Prince Hotel's garden, April 20th, 1975

them to the others for enhancement or even the guillotine. It was not often an ideal situation, as a sense of togetherness was sometimes lost when one or other of them were working in separate studios. There was never a lack of ideas, however, which simply fountained from their brains.

This method was never more evident than in one of the five songs on the album that Freddie had written, which had a very sweet working title; "*Fred's Thing*". He had put together all of the piano, bass and drum parts, including vocal arrangements, pieced together day by day. Each band member recorded their instruments but had no inkling how their contributions would be slotted in or mixed. Freddie had also taken inspiration from the light comic operas of Gilbert and Sullivan and had incorporated his ideas into the song using an operatic section that was intended to connect the melodic and rock sections of the song. The operatic section became extended, as did the song, which had twice the length of a normal pop song. Only when it was near completion did it acquire it's legendary name: 'Bohemian Rhapsody'.

Its recording was also legendary, with stories of the original tape being round past the heads of the tape player so often — as Freddie added yet one more "*Galileo*" and each individual vocal harmony was bounced to another track before the next was recorded — that it wore so thin you could "*see through it*" according to May.

With the bulk of the recording over so was the search for an album name, and it was the Marx Brothers film from 1935 that inspired it; a Night At The Opera. The band adjourned from Rockfield Studios near Monmouth in Wales, and descended on Scorpio Studios and Sarn East for the overdubbing. Freddie left nothing to chance and nor did Brian, who allegedly spent a week perfecting a guitar solo; their perfectionism was legendary and impressive.

As was Bohemian Rhapsody, although, worryingly, it left those who first heard the finished version gobsmacked but confused. Undaunted, Freddie declared that it was going to be the next single. It was a very bold move for a band that knew, after all that had happened, that it was possibly looking into the abyss. Bohemian Rhapsody elicited the same swearing and disbelief from the EMI men in grey suits. It would never get near a BBC turntable at that length they argued; it was 5 minutes 55 seconds long.

However, they won over a valuable ally; one of Capital Radio's top DJs Kenny Everett in London, who listened to it and thought that the band had a hit on their hands. He even played a few seconds on his show as a teaser and then unleashed it fourteen times on his listeners during one weekend. Everett and Freddie would become good friends.

EMI no longer had a leg to stand on; the BBC had played the song.

It was time to go off on tour again; twenty-four venues starting on the 4th of November at the Liverpool Empire before sweeping back to the USA, with fingers crossed no doubt, then on to Japan and ending in Australia. Fans would be treated to a barrage of lights, magnesium flares and dry ice and Freddie, the pièce de résistance, magnificent in a panorama of, amongst other things, satin, a Japanese kimono and white wings by Hermès.

Bohemian Rhapsody, of course, was too complicated to sing live in its entirety, and the workaround in later concerts was for the operatic middle section to be played on tape, whilst the band left the stage.

Bohemian Rhapsody was fired out into the world via the BBC on Top of the Pops on the 20th of November 1975. One day later, a Night At The Opera surged out into the shops. It was the band's coup d'état and contains some extraordinary tracks,

one of which was Brian May's track 'The Prophet's Song', a huge composition lasting eight minutes. It was born of a dream about a great flood, which he'd had whilst he was recovering from his illness. And although the band disliked trying to explain the meaning of songs — Bohemian Rhapsody still remains an enigma — 'Love of My Life' is straightforward being a love song to Freddie's girlfriend, Mary Austin, and became one of his most popular and most covered songs.

The album was a huge success, despite the ambivalence of some of the reviews in the American music press (there were no press reviews for the UK album release); "*Achieves a parodic tone often enough to suggest more than meets the ear*". AllMusic would later write that it was a "*self-consciously ridiculous and overblown hard-rock masterpiece*". But there was plenty of praise, too, with the album "*full of great songwriting and prog influences*".

But there was no doubt what the fans thought; on November 25th, Bohemian Rhapsody had struck the gong for the band; it was at number 1 in the UK charts and would remain in the charts for seventeen weeks. And A Night At The Opera would also go to number 1 in the UK and three other countries. Queen had a huge success on their hands. The gamble they had taken in resisting the doubters, their persistence and belief in themselves, had turned to gold.

The tour continued through the UK with a show on the 24th of December at the Hammersmith Odeon in London followed by almost four weeks of rest before the American leg began on the 24th of January.

Time, perhaps, for Freddie to take stock of his personal life. It was as though he were two different people, the extrovert on stage decked out with nail polish and furs and slinging "*darlings*" around, and the sensitive man off stage struggling with his sexuality. That sensitivity would become apparent whenever Freddie was unable to control his environment, at parties that were not for him, for example, a sensation he always loathed as it left him feeling shy and vulnerable.

Freddie had met David Minns in early 1975, a record executive, 25 years old, and the two had become lovers. Yet Mary Austin was still a feature of his life and still lived with him and slept in the same bed. The effects of Bohemian Rhapsody rippled into his personal life, too. Mary noticed that their relationship had begun to cool; indeed, as the end of 1976 approached, the relationship as it had been would be over forever. Freddie left the flat they shared, but the depth of his feelings for her was evident when he bought her a £30,000 apartment in London, and she would eventually work for Goose Productions, Freddie's own production company. The deep friendship that had bonded them for so long would endure, however, surviving practically all of his other relationships. A new life beckoned Freddie; it was as though his success had emboldened him to show the world what he truly was, and the message buried within the tale of his struggles that was Bohemian Rhapsody was that change was taking place. The prima donna inside was being released of any constraints, and if any proof were needed, it came during the gig in Australia Sydney on the 17th of April 1976 when Freddie refused to walk to the venue on foot and later, consumed with anger, smashed a mirror over the head of Pete Brown, the band's coordinator. An out-of-control Freddie could be a dangerous beast; "*I've created a monster*", he said of himself. But he could not restrain its appetites.

And then they were off to the US, where they would tour from the end of January to the 13th of March 1976 taking in a four-venue stop in New York along the way. The reception was far different than it had been on previous tours, marked by the fact that Freddie was now a major pop star, who was permitted to cover his shyness at after show parties with tantrums and by flouncing away, ostensibly because people he did not like were

LEFT: Queen at Les Ambassadeurs where they were presented with silver, gold and platinum discs for sales in excess of one million of their hit single 'Bohemian Rhapsody'

MAIN IMAGE: Queen strolling in a Japanese garden, Tokyo, March 21, 1976

present — executives, journalists or hangers on. On stage or in front of an interviewer's camera, Freddie had no qualms about taking the spotlight.

With Bohemian Rhapsody being pushed up the charts, where it would eventually reach number 9, the US press, too, though classing Queen as a European creation, i.e., not quite suitable for American tastes, were on the band's side and foresaw 10,000-seater venues for their next tour of the States. And so, without mishap this time, the tour concluded at San Diego Sports Arena giving them just over one week before the start of an eight-venue tour in Japan.

JAPAN LOVED THEM EVEN MORE THE SECOND TIME AROUND.

And Freddie particularly loved the shopping, in which, having money, he could now indulge himself, diving into shops kept empty for him, sometimes with the Japanese promoter's wife in tow. Freddie was in his element, buying clothes, furniture and artwork for shipping back to the United Kingdom.

How would audiences react on the final leg of their tour in Australia in April? After the difficulties of the first tour, this one had practically sold out all the venues in the big towns.

A very successful period was rewarded by a three-month break at the end of the Australian leg of the tour, and the satisfaction of seeing their single 'You're My Best Friend', written by John Deacon, go to number 7 in the UK charts.

Keen to keep the momentum after another success, they plunged back into work on another album in July, which they produced themselves. The challenge now was to follow up a successful A Night at the Opera and still sound fresh and inventive. Pressure would be released in some spectacular

RIGHT: Brian May and lead singer Freddie Mercury performing live, 1977 in Boston

rows, with Freddie holding the title of Row Maker in Chief, but it was always with one aim; the pursuit of perfection in the music.

A Day at the Races, the new album, began to fall behind schedule and would only finally see the light of day in December, spawning three singles; another Queen classic, 'Somebody to Love', which was released on November the 12th 1976 and hit number 2 in the UK charts; it was followed in March 1977 by 'Tie Your Mother Down', which got to number 31, and then in May, 'Good Old Fashioned Lover Boy', which climbed to number 17.

Before then there would be two grand events; one was Freddie's 30th birthday; 150 guests were invited to shell lobster and crystal champagne in the King's Road; the second took place in Hyde Park, where a show was staged on the 6th anniversary of Jimi Hendrix's demise in which Queen headlined with an hour-long show in front of 150,000 people. Freddie, who had been secretly brought into the park in the back of a laundry van, was a bag of nerves, spitting abuse at the hangers-on backstage. The concert's success was tempered by a police threat to arrest Freddie if he went on stage again having broken a police curfew when Queen overran by thirty minutes. It mattered not, and the release of A Day at the Races heralded the end of a decade in which Queen were rapidly approaching their dream scenario; "*To be the biggest band in the world*".

The pop rock of A Day at the Races found favour with some critics and many fans: except the New musical Express. The NME in the mid-70s saw itself as the champion of punk and was railing against the big production bands like Pink Floyd and especially Queen, who came in for some first-rate abuse in the reviews; "*Cutie-pie mirror-preening essence of ultra preciousness*";"*Grotesquery of the first order*", it howled. Rolling Stone was little better, accusing Mercury of having nothing more than a "*passable pop voice*". It mattered little, because

the album was a number one hit in the UK — and, naturally, in Japan — and rose to number 5 in the US.

'Somebody to Love' was in many respects a sibling to 'Bohemian Rhapsody' incorporating complex layers of vocal tracks, intricate harmonies and a Brian May guitar solo. Mercury had been inspired by gospel music, Aretha Franklin in particular, and he, Brian, Roger and John created a 100-voice gospel choir by multi-tracking their own voices. "*This wasn't just rock and roll*", said writer Mark Blake. It wasn't. It was also a baroque masterpiece, and Brian May was the first to credit Freddie for the extraordinary creative input by the singer on the album.

So the new year of 1977, notwithstanding the sudden eruption of the Sex Pistols, saw Queen buoyed by the heat of their very own volcano, and by the 13th of January, they were back in the US and Canada on a tour to support the album. The opening act for most of the venues was Thin Lizzy, and the New York venue sold out within minutes of tickets going on sale. It did not remain the only sold-out venue.

Freddie's personality had gained another trait in the meantime, suspicion, because everybody wanted something from him. Freddie, was now indulged by a football team of assistants, sycophants and hangers-on, and he ruled the roost as far as what Queen would or wouldn't do was concerned; and his demands were manifold, his every need was catered for whatever the consequence for others; he wouldn't allow freezing fans into the auditorium in Chicago until the soundcheck was over, and the tour also marked the end of the presence of David Minns in Freddie's life. The glamorous freedom offered by this new lifestyle was embraced by the singer wholeheartedly, and boys trailed up to his hotel rooms. There was no doubt that the band knew he was gay, and it couldn't have been less important to them. Each musician enjoyed his own private life away from the others, with John accompanied by his wife and son, and earnest Brian by his

LEFT: Freddie Mercury live in New Haven, 1977

super brain that needed to be fed with information at all times.

Two months after the start of the American tour, the band were in Europe for another eight concerts, returning to England for eleven more and finally coming to a standstill on the 7th of June having been on the road since the 13th of January with a break during April.

IT WAS TIME FOR A CHANGE.

Brian later confessed that the last two albums had indeed probably been overproduced, and Roger Taylor was also eager to make an album that was less complex and more in tune with an era that was lauding the Sex Pistols.

So, just a short time after ending the tour, they were due in the studio again to work on their 6th album. And with Taylor anxious to get going, a two month cut-off time for recording had been set and a November tour arranged to make sure that there was no other choice but to get it done. Brian was not particularly happy about touring again so soon, because of the difficulties this brought to maintaining his relationship with Chrissy, especially as they were expecting their first child, and while Roger had been involved with Dominique Beyrand ever since they had met at the Hyde Park concert the year before, he was still keen to go back out on the road. Roger and Dominique would live together until 1987 and have two children. Freddie, too, was eager to get out into the world with his latest lover, the "sweet and naive" Joe Fanelli, in tow. John's wife, Veronica, was also pregnant.

Work began on the album, to be co-produced by Queen and Mike Stone, in July. It would not be called Duck Soup, apparently because Groucho Marx objected, and so it was re-christened News of the World.

The band shifted their sound away from the progressive rock emphasis of previous albums and tried to achieve a more mainstream sound experimenting from soft rock to hard rock. It wasn't to everyone's liking in the music press, one reviewer mocking some of the songs about "the futile rebelliousness of the doomed-to-life losers", but the band composed several very successful songs, two of which were destined to become anthems the world over; 'We Will Rock You', from the pen of Brian May and 'We Are the Champions' from Freddie. 'Spread Your Wings', by John Deacon, also had a very healthy chart run.

With 'We Will Rock You', Brian had written what became one of Queen's biggest worldwide successes, once it had found its way into the raucous chants of the sports arenas. Brian had intentionally made the song simplistic and anthemic so that the audiences would have a chance to join in with the singing; and it fulfilled that purpose beyond his wildest expectations.

Freddie, too, had excelled himself when he wrote 'We Are The Champions', the "most egotistical song I've ever written", according to Freddie. May was "quite shocked" with the lyrics and concerned about the seeming self-praise that positively oozed from them, and it would mean that forever after, May and Taylor would be defending themselves, saying the song referred to the band as a collective and not to their superiority over others. Nonetheless, the New York Yankees adopted the song as their anthem, and the fans sent it to no 2 in the UK and 4 in the US.

Just after the album recording was finished, Queen received the Britannia Award for the best British single of the last 25 years (together With 'A Whiter Shade of Pale' by Procol Harum) for 'Bohemian Rhapsody'.

The song written by John Deacon, 'Spread Your Wings', the first Queen song without backing vocals, concerns Sammy, a troubled young man sweeping the floor in a bar. The advice given to him in Freddie Mercury's vocals is to "spread your

MAIN IMAGE: Madison Square Garden, 1977

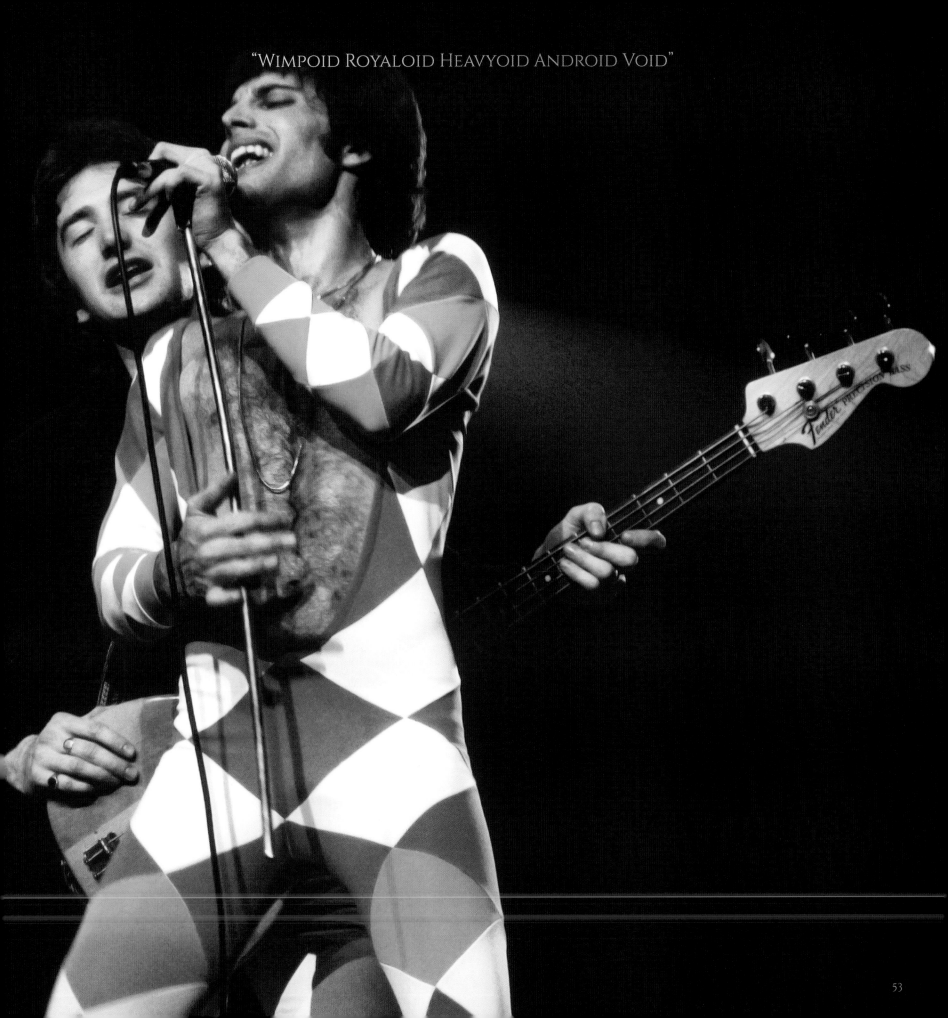

wings and fly away". The song got a number 34 in the UK.

'It's Late' was also written by Brian May but fared much less well in the charts. It was one of the "*these things happen in life*" songs about a complicated love life with two women, which Brian described as being "*about all sorts of experiences that I had, and experiences that I thought other people had, but I guess it was very personal*". He wrote it in three parts and also used the tapping technique that Van Halen and Steve Hackett were known for.

The album went to number 4 in the UK and 3 in the US, and it also reached number 1 in both Holland and France. Lukewarm reviews or not, by veering off in a radical new direction, the News of the World had saved Queen from being rolled over and sidelined by the punk wave as other bands had been.

Following a concert in London in October, they were back off to reconquer America, opening in Portland on the 11th of November with gigs through until the 22nd of December; the tour was the first the band had been on without an opening act.

Whilst not averse to its pleasures, American critics were still somewhat baffled by Queen's music, which defied categorisation, but for the audiences, their colourful exuberance won them over every time, although Freddie's vocalised haughty contempt for them often strayed dangerously close to the line.

Success, however, brought with it new problems such as the 83% income tax in the United Kingdom and a conflict of interests with their manager John Reid, who also managed Elton John. A solution to the second problem was easily found by dispensing John's services, and he then received 15% of the royalties on Queen albums up to that date in compensation for the early termination of his contract.

The band decided to manage themselves, but fortunately for them, before long, the lawyer who had negotiated that separation, Jim Beach, had become the band's business manager, and one of his first acts was to renegotiate the deal with EMI; the terms of the renegotiated million-pound deal were extremely favourable to Queen. Which made the first problem even more pressing; the solution to this was more complex and required the group to become tax exiles, as many famous musicians had done before them — which meant not spending more than 183 days in the UK. Amongst all of this business activity, John Deacon was the band's eye on the money, keeping a close watch on their business affairs and advising the others on what was going on.

1977 drew to a close amidst this atmosphere of change, and the band finished their News of the World Tour, that "*most spectacularly staged and finely honed show*", as one American reviewer described it, and flew home for Christmas. The band would not tour again until the following April, when they would set off on the European leg. In the meantime, they settled into their own, often very different lives, coming together for rehearsals, concerts and meetings, but arriving and leaving separately.

ALL A FAR CRY FROM THE EARLIER DAYS OF SQUEEZING INTO ONE VAN.

MAIN IMAGE: Madison Square Garden, 1978

Freddie always needed companionship and enjoyed an expanded circle of gay friends, some of whom were more loyal than others. And he was determined to live life to the full, drinking in all the trappings of stardom, boasting of £100,000 spent over three years, and exploiting the eagerness of his fawning hangers-on. His days extended into late nights and early mornings; Freddie's life was fast-paced and all-encompassing.

Brian's was the opposite and revolved around family life — Chrissy and Brian's first child, James, was born in June 1978 — and there was no outward display of stardom; Brian, lived in a modest detached house in Barnes in London.

John Deacon was the polar opposite of Freddie, a man who did not really enjoy the celebrity lifestyle, rarely gave interviews and preferred the company of his close friends and family.

Roger Taylor was more on Freddie's wavelength; "*Freddie Mercury and I both loved to have a laugh on tour. If there were shenanigans and good times, Fred and I would be there*", the drummer is quoted as saying many years later. Roger also loved the glamour, the cars and country houses that went with being a rockstar.

In the summer of 1978, the band reconvened to work on their seventh studio album, Jazz, a project that saw Roy Thomas Baker replacing producer Mike Stone; Baker was thrilled to be working with Freddie again, and the album emerged with a variety of musical styles that brought the boys praise and the usual rounds of criticism. The implications of their tax situation had kicked in, and Brian had left the UK to avoid the punitive tax regime shortly after the birth of James, and the band yo-yoed between studios in Nice in the south of France and Mountain Studios on Lake Geneva. The release

of the album would also finally see them released from their contractual obligations to Trident.

Once again, each of the musicians' songwriting talents was on display, with the lion's share going to Freddie, who kicked off the album with his track 'Mustapha', wandering into territory reserved for Arabic music and being gloriously camp and gloriously exuberant. Mercury's lyrics were made up of English, Arabic, Persian and very probably a series of invented words.

May's contributions roamed between light jazz and heavy rock, between 'Leaving Home Ain't Easy' and 'Dead On Time' in which May incorporates some of his fastest and most aggressive guitar playing, backed by Taylor's intense drumming. And Mercury twice reaches up to the C#5 note. Elsewhere May's superb guitar could be heard in a solo on Deacon's other song, 'If You Can't Beat Them'.

One of Deacon's contributions, 'In Only Seven Days', was chosen as the B-side to 'Don't Stop Me Now', written by Mercury. Freddie's upbeat lyrics and uplifting beat on that track came home at a satisfactory number 9 in the UK and became one of Queen's most famous songs. 'Fat Bottomed Girls' and 'Bicycle Race' were also issued on a single and nestled in at number 11 in the UK. Ever on the lookout for something new, the band wanted the video to involve sixty-five naked female models of all races and sizes cycling around Wimbledon Stadium in London.

Jazz seemed to lack a sense of cohesion; Roger Taylor belittled his own contributions calling them instantly forgettable and adding that as they were all living in different countries there had been much less of a group sense of community than they had been used to. It was generally disappointing to them; and it was torched by a review in the Rolling Stone, which even called them fascist, sexist tax

RIGHT: Queen, 1978

exiles. Readers in the NME were urged not to buy it unless they had a deaf relative. In later years, reviewers would be less severe and fans still considered it an excellent album; so it reached number 2 in the UK and 6 in the US.

But it was Freddie's free-roaming lifestyle that at that moment in time was worrying his fellow bandmates most of all. Success had transformed the singer into a panther out of its cage, and he became a one-man drugs and sex show with seemingly limitless uncontainable energy and insatiable urges. Problems with his voice resurfaced, which he blamed on nodules although his lifestyle certainly didn't help.

But the show had to go on, so, despite Freddie's voice being under par — not helped by the fact that the tour to promote the album began in the same month as the recording sessions finished on Jazz — at the end of October 1978, the tour began in Dallas USA. Freddie's voice wasn't able to recover sufficiently, and the result was a less powerful performances then he would normally have given on a tour that would continue through until the first week of May 1979, when it ended in Japan having passed through Europe in January and February.

Freddie's image, though, belied the strain on his voice as he adopted biker's trousers, jacket and cap and topped it all off with a big chain necklace. Everyone else remained the same, the angelic Roger and Brian, and John the Quiet sitting upright in his shirt and tie.

The European leg would be filmed for a live album release, Live Killers, their first, which EMI had wanted them to do, lacking an immediate follow-up to Jazz. It couldn't match the sound quality of their pedantic studio projects and without visuals was lacking an important dimension of their live shows, but the energy and drive were still apparent.

The final show was in Germany in August, cast adrift from the main body of the tour that had finished in May. One month later, Freddie was 33-years old. Despite his inability to be faithful, friends insisted that what he wanted most of all was a stable relationship. Perhaps he hoped to have found it later in the year when he moved a man called Tony Bastin into his London home. The relationship lasted but a few months.

One month further on again from Freddie's birthday, and EMI, who were pleased with 'Crazy Little Thing Called Love', rushed out the single for October complete with a video in which the boys were all clad in black leather. Freddie's talent for the unusual, his push to achieve what was extravagant and even unsettling, had struck gold again, and the single went to Number 2 in the UK and number one on the US Billboard hot 100 and in 3 other countries.

The band decided to follow up the single with a short tour in Britain and Ireland, to begin in the middle of November and run through to Boxing Day, December the 26th, 1979. The Crazy Tour has gone down in the diaries of fans as one of the best Queen ever undertook. Freddie's vocal chords had recovered from whatever problems he had been experiencing and his voice might well have been better than it had ever been before in live performances. His own confidence in his vocal abilities led to him experiment more freely and soar up to high notes that he'd never dared to attempt in a live setting before. What may also have helped was the decision to stage the shows in many smaller venues of just two thousand seats, with the exception of Dublin and Birmingham, in an attempt to change the dynamic of the full-on larger stagings.

In January, as the new decade of the 1980s broke, Queen's single 'Save Me' was on its climb to number 11 in the UK, another notch in their own successful rise, which brought with

MAIN IMAGE: Freddie Mercury gets training from a
ballet instructor, August 1979

it pressures to keep on producing. By February they were back in the studios in Munich, where they spent four months working on the next album, the longest time they had ever spent on recording sessions in one place. And it paid off, as perhaps as many as forty songs flowed from those sessions, Freddie and Brian writing for all they were worth. Ideas were balanced between Freddie, Brian and Roger as they hummed and sang their melody lines and harmonies to one another discussing and altering.

John preferred to create a song alone, only presenting the finished product to his bandmates. And on one occasion, John produced pure gold by writing 'Another One Bites the Dust', an infectious disco number. Freddie loved it and the singing style involved. Roger resisted; it wasn't rock 'n' roll and he didn't want it as a single. Fortunately, he didn't prevail, and John then played almost all instruments on the recording, the bass guitar, piano, and the handclaps. When it was released later in the year, the song was number 1 on the US Billboard Hot 100 for three weeks and number 2 on the Hot Soul and Hot Disco charts. That wasn't all; it was a hit worldwide, and stayed for fifteen weeks in the Billboard Top Ten to become the longest running top ten song of 1980, 31 weeks total on the chart, a record for 1980. It was number 7 on the UK Singles Chart. It would become Queen's best-selling single, sales totalling over 7 million copies.

Each of the band members' different musical directions vied for attention on the final product, and the songs veered from heavy rock to disco, pop to ballads and on to rockabilly, whilst for the first time ever, a synthesiser found its way onto a Queen album; an Oberheim OB-X. Many things were different, including the fact that with producer and engineer, Reinhold Mack's encouragement, many of the vocal tracks would be one take only.

Staying in one place for too long would bring problems

for this restless band, however. To break up the recording routines and relax, cocktails would be mixed at 6 o'clock and more alcohol served before dinner, after which everyone would fan out to their own favourite night spots before repairing back to the Hilton Hotel in Munich, where they would hang out in one or other of the suites rented by the band. When they did finally get to bed, it was so late that no one got up for breakfast before the afternoon. Freddie's voice and performances were not unaffected by these riotous outings.

Tensions snaked through the sessions, with disagreements on which songs to release as singles, the majority of violent disagreements flaring between Roger and Brian the perfectionist, who preferred to forgo the pleasures of Munich night life for late nights in the studio. The music was always at the heart of these conflicts that were flecked with such stories as the one where Brian walked out of the studio one day in anger.

The fun and games were over in May, the month that Roger became a father when Dominique gave birth to Felix. Taylor would also produce his debut solo album, which he worked on during a break in the next tour. It would be called Fun in Space, ten tracks on which he played all the instruments and sang. Taylor would also use synthesisers, which the group had hitherto refused to use, but which had made an appearance on the new album Game. When Fun in Space was released in April 1981, it got to number 18 in the UK charts. Taylor would make a further four solo albums; Strange Frontier, 1984, Happiness, 1994, Electric Fire, 1998 and Fun on Earth, 2013.

The new album, Game, appeared on the streets on the 30th of June 1980. It became their best-selling album in the US going straight to number 1 and repeating the trick in the UK. As ever, reviewers were in two minds; "*Queen are the most*

exciting band I've ever seen or heard", commented one, to be countered by a dismissive, "*sandwiched between two slabs of Queen's usual symphonic and/or choral pomp-rock... lies a filling of utterly unoriginal corn*".

Whilst he was a tax exile abroad, Freddie had asked Mary, the woman he would always call his best friend, to find him a new house in London. She came up with Garden Lodge, 1 Logan Place, a Georgian mansion with eight bedrooms. Freddie adored it from the moment he saw it and for £500,000 in cash it was his. It was a significant purchase and was going to be his last residence. High brick walls shielded him from the outside world, proving that in contradiction to his flamboyant public persona, at home Freddie wanted a private and secluded life.

There would not be much chance to enjoy privacy and seclusion in the year to come; the band would begin their next tour in support of Game at the end of June 1980, and it would run through to March 1981 before recommencing in August the same year, ending in November.

It was, apparently, after a concert in Los Angeles that Michael Jackson suggested to the band that 'Another One Bites the Dust' should be released as a single. After hitting the number 1 spot on the US Billboard Hot 100, it remained in the top five for thirteen weeks and was in the charts for thirty-one weeks in total, eventually achieving multi-platinum status.

Between the ending of three shows in New York City on the 30th of September and the start of the European leg of the tour in November, the band went back into the recording studio to compose the soundtrack for a science fiction movie that would become a cult classic; Flash Gordon. It turned into somewhat of a marathon, especially for Brian, who was left to pick up the pieces at the end. Roger was full of

RIGHT: Queen live at the Groenoordhallen in Leiden, Netherlands, 27th November 1980

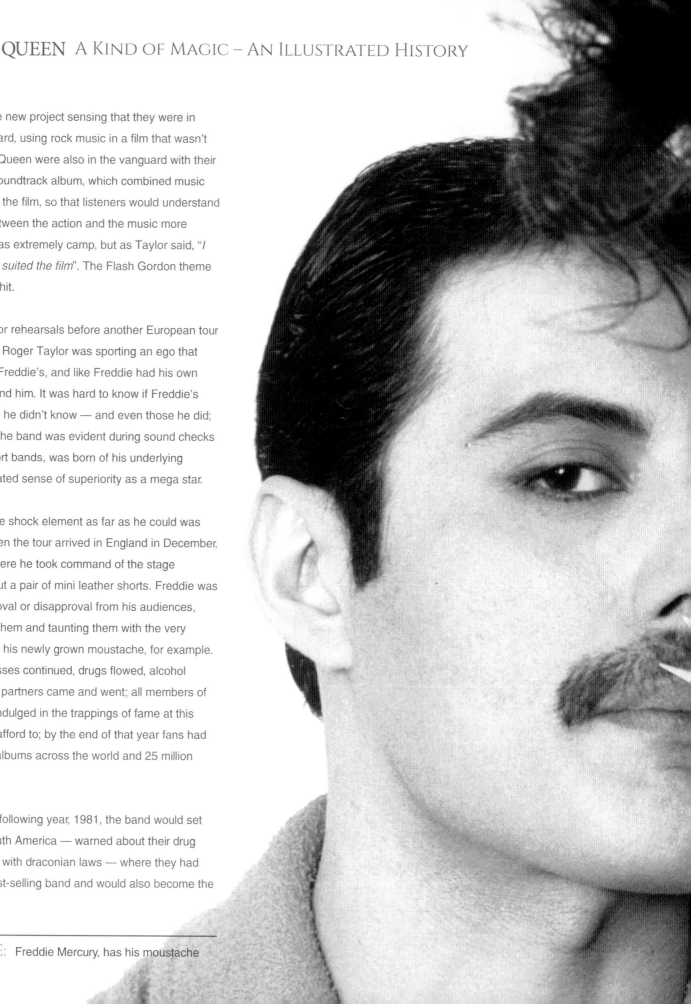

enthusiasm for the new project sensing that they were in the cultural vanguard, using rock music in a film that wasn't about musicians. Queen were also in the vanguard with their treatment of the soundtrack album, which combined music and dialogue from the film, so that listeners would understand the connection between the action and the music more readily. The film was extremely camp, but as Taylor said, "*I thought our music suited the film*". The Flash Gordon theme became a top ten hit.

Then it was time for rehearsals before another European tour kicked off. By now Roger Taylor was sporting an ego that wasn't far behind Freddie's, and like Freddie had his own set of friends around him. It was hard to know if Freddie's aloofness to those he didn't know — and even those he did; his distance from the band was evident during sound checks — including support bands, was born of his underlying shyness or an inflated sense of superiority as a mega star.

His urge to take the shock element as far as he could was given free rein when the tour arrived in England in December, in Birmingham, where he took command of the stage wearing nothing but a pair of mini leather shorts. Freddie was indifferent to approval or disapproval from his audiences, often swearing at them and taunting them with the very thing they disliked; his newly grown moustache, for example. Offstage the excesses continued, drugs flowed, alcohol flowed and sexual partners came and went; all members of the band happily indulged in the trappings of fame at this point. They could afford to; by the end of that year fans had bought 45 million albums across the world and 25 million singles.

In February of the following year, 1981, the band would set off for dates in South America — warned about their drug intake in a country with draconian laws — where they had become the biggest-selling band and would also become the

MAIN IMAGE: Freddie Mercury, has his moustache groomed, 1982

first to play in major stadia. A problem in itself, as they had to provide artificial turf so that the football pitches wouldn't be damaged. It became a logistical nightmare to move the over 100 tons of equipment and co-ordinate the many people, shady or otherwise, involved.

The audience numbers were astonishing, however; in Buenos Aires a crowd of over 300,000 were present, the largest single concert crowd ever in Argentine history. São Paulo in Brazil saw huge audience numbers on two consecutive nights; six of the eight performances scheduled in Mexico had to be cancelled, however.

The media accompanied Queen wherever they went, and they were escorted in armoured vehicles by motorcycle police clearing the way with sirens. They were even escorted onto the stage by armed soldiers.

Freddie was dressed for the occasion in a white, sleeveless Superman T-shirt, red vinyl pants and a black vinyl jacket and would often stop singing to allow the audience their chance to join in; and the fans, it appeared, knew all the lyrics, as the boys sailed through the 110 minutes concert with 'Keep Yourself Alive', 'Killer Queen', 'Bohemian Rhapsody', 'Fat Bottomed Girls' or 'Bicycle Race'.

Their reward for being good boys was dinner with Argentinian President General Roberto Eduardo Viola, although the glamour didn't help him as he was ousted in a military coup that December. Queen, however, came out of the experience, $3.5 million richer and having trumped rival bands, something they were always keen to do on the way to being the biggest band on the planet. Indeed, Queen were, as Brian May put it, "*the biggest thing in the world for a moment in time*", adding, "*and everything that goes with that really messes up your mind somehow. We've all suffered. Freddie, obviously, went completely AWOL... He was utterly out of control... it screwed us up*".

The band would return to South America in September. In the meantime, they went to Switzerland and Mountain Studios. Brian joined them shortly after Chrissy had given birth to their daughter Louisa.

One of the highlights of the recording sessions took place in July when David Bowie turned up to record his song 'Cat People (Putting Out Fire)'. The jamming sessions they all started, ended with collaboration on a song that was finally baptised 'Under Pressure', a Bowie suggestion, and it was Bowie who took over the sessions, despite heightened sensitivity by a band used to having its own way. Freddie and David engaged in fierce discussions as did Brian May, who eventually gave up trying, with Roger Taylor attempting to keep the peace. Bowie had decided that they should all sing the melody separately, in any way they wanted, in the recording booth, from which eventually emerged Freddie Mercury's unique introduction. It may have had a difficult birth, but Queen played it at all their live concerts from then until 1986. Released in October, it went to number 1 in the UK and three other territories to acclaim by critics, one of whom dubbed it as "*the best song of all time*", and the bass line, which John Deacon said was Bowie's child, as "*the best in popular music history*".

But then the summer was over and they headed for New Orleans and rehearsals prior to returning to South America. It was when they got to Mexico that the trouble started.

By this time they were used to passing dollars to enable people and equipment to pass from one place to another, but Mexico did its best to top every other country. The first concert passed off without incident until the bridge outside the stadium collapsed and the band found themselves locked inside the stadium until dollars set them free. But at the next

gig with the crowd fuelled by tequila and mescaline, the stage was soon littered with the debris thrown onto it. The band got through to the end, but were so furious they wanted to go home straight away. They were persuaded to complete a third gig, which went more smoothly, but then they got out as fast as they could with the trucks driven back to United States with an armed guard.

It had been a salutary experience that made them realise they were not invincible and thinking that they were could lose them serious amounts of money.

Ruffled feathers were soothed with the success of 'Under Pressure', which was also included in the release of their Greatest Hits album on the 26th of October. It hit the number one spot in the UK, where it stayed for four weeks, and four other countries, and in total spent 800 weeks in the UK charts, the best-selling album of all time, eventually clocking up sales of over 25 million copies worldwide, to reviews that were full of praise.

Another distraction from the shock of Mexico was the studio in Munich, where they reassembled in December to continue sessions for a new album. It was given the title Hot Space.

It was though Mexico had started a period of heavy waves for the band; Freddie Mercury was perceived by the others as becoming too reliant on his manager, Paul Prenter, who they felt was segregating Freddie from them. Freddie wanted to move in a new direction, more funky, "*less guitar*" and less heavy production, and the result was not at all to Roger and Brian's liking. With drugs and alcohol in abundance, late nights extended into mornings and the work suffered. None of the band were to escape the emotional turmoil of a lifestyle that was out of control. Freddie, as usual, seemed to be at the head of the queue for strife, and brought his rows with his new lover, an American, Bill Reid, into the studio.

MAIN IMAGE: Brian May, John Deacon, Roger Taylor and Freddie Mercury, pose for group portrait, 1982

Brian and Freddie created three songs apiece, and Deacon and Mercury collaborated on a soul number, 'Cool Cat'. Brian rebelled against the relentless funk, and bitter arguments with Roger flared up when Roger said he didn't like what Brian was doing on his guitar in Roger's songs. Whatever his own tribulations, Freddie was a wonderful no-nonsense arbitrator between the other band members when the sessions dragged on for so long that even Mack despaired they would ever end, or feared that the band would disintegrate before the end was reached.

Incorporating many elements of disco, funk, rhythm and blues, dance and pop music was not to Roger or Brian's liking at all; nor was the decided musical slant towards gay that Freddie was giving it, which Brian deemed to be non-inclusive. Brian was all but non-existent on the first side of the album, with John and Freddie's soul and funk to the fore. Brian's mood showed in the video of the single selected to demonstrate Queen's Brave New World to it's fans; Freddie's, 'Body Language'. Americans were happy with it, the Brits not so much; it didn't quite make the top 20 in the UK. The video for the single had the distinction of being banned by MTV thanks to the areas of bare female flesh involved.

Hot Space, which went on to the streets on the 21st of May 1982, became one of the fans' least favourite albums, even though Michael Jackson is quoted as saying that it was the inspiration for his Thriller album. Nonetheless, it got to number 4 in the UK though faring less well in the States at number 22 on the U.S billboard 200. There was no doubt that it was their most experimental album to date. No one else sang with Freddie, for a start, who handled the vocals alone .

Freddie's 'Staying Power' replete with horns and Michael Jackson-like squeals failed to chart as a single as did John Deacon's 'Back Chat' although it did get to number 3 in France; Brian, who had fought hard to keep the rock elements in the music, might have been permitted a small smile. He managed to get some rock in on his own compositions 'Dancer' and 'Put Out the Fire', with 'Las Palabras de Amor' returning to musical hunting grounds that Brian would have been happy with, which the band sang on Top of the Pops for the first live appearance in five years.

The music press were disappointed for the most part and dismissive of the rock band that had "*lost the plot*" and the sound that allowed Brian's guitar merely "*as flavour only on occasion*".

YET, WHEN MICHAEL JACKSON CAME UP WITH THRILLER, IT SEEMED AS THOUGH QUEEN HAD, IN FACT, BEEN AHEAD OF THEIR TIME.

LEFT: Queen live at Tokorozawa Seibu Lion's Baseball Stadium, Saitama, November 3, 1982

The tour to support the album was already underway by the time the album came out, having started in April. A mammoth run through to November was planned, starting off this time in Europe. Three cancelled dates in America gave them over one month free, however, from the middle of September. Musically, they tumbled around the genres they had covered, from pomp rock and heavy metal to funk and gospel; it didn't all go smoothly. Unhappy with some of the new material, there were jeers from the German audience, which was smartly told by Freddie that if they didn't like it they could "**** *go home!*" Even the first support band Bow Wow Wow were the targets of bottles hurled onto the stage. Fans in England, too, were quick to voice their disapproval of the support acts.

Queen set off for the American leg of the tour; it had occurred to Roger Taylor that they were not "*packing them in quite as much as we used to*", which made him grateful for their support act there, Billy Squier, an American rock musician, who was at that point enjoying a spurt in his fame. Billy was a Queen fan and admirer of Freddie, and he too had noticed that audiences had become unsure about this new version of Queen; was it all a big joke? Were they being taken for a ride?

Freddie, in his personal life, was causing the same questions to be asked; he was being treated as he wished, like the Sun King, spoon feeding and all, surrounded by sycophants and shielded from even his bandmates by the all-powerful Paul Prenter. Freddie's arguments with his boyfriend Bill Reid could turn into physical violence anywhere, and he was just as liable to subject those around him to sudden irrational tirades; part of the problem was that he was growing bored with touring.

As for the others, increasingly remote from their flamboyant frontman, life was more about trying to balance work and home and family life, and the strain often showed in the tension onstage as well as off.

Life as a member of the mega band Queen was changing, although no one could know it, but when they headed away from their final concert in America in Los Angeles, America would never see Queen and Freddie Mercury together again. Before long, Queen would also leave record company Elektra and sign for EMI/Capitol Records. Elektra gained $1 million for agreeing to give up on their existing deal with the band. Freddie was going to sign a deal with CBS and Columbia for a one-off solo project.

America may have fallen out of love with them, but the icing on the cake of the tour would be the last dates in Japan, a country that had always welcomed them and treated them like royalty, even though Hot Space only made it to number 6 on the Japanese charts. Nonetheless, when it was over, everyone was glad to be rid of the others and to go back to their separate lives. The animosity between them persisted for sometime afterwards.

A big change in Freddie's life now came with his move to New York, where he began a new life at East 5th Street. Accompanied by his "*New York daughters*" as he called them, four friends, he could now be seen frequenting the clubs and bars of his adopted city — by now, Bill Reid had been relegated to history.

As the band had decided not to do more live performances in 1983, Roger and Brian used the early months of that year to pursue their own projects, Roger heading back to Mountain Studios to work at his second solo album, Strange Frontier, whilst Brian flew to Los Angeles to work on an album of his own. On the 21st and 22nd of April, Brian, together with Roger, guitarist Eddie Van Halen, drummer Alan Gratzer, bass player Phil Chen and keyboard player Fred Mandel, had

RIGHT: Roger Taylor attends a fashion night by Alan Price at the Camden Palace in London, 1983

a jamming session in the studio. Originally, it wasn't intended for release, but Brian finally gave in to pressure from friends who had heard the music and Star Fleet Project was sent out into the world in October 1983. There were just three tracks on it: 'Star Fleet', 'Let Me Out', and 'Blues Breaker' dedicated to Eric Clapton. It was a delight for guitar fans everywhere.

Freddie was involved in composing some music for a soundtrack for the Metropolis film made in 1926 but intended for re-release. He, too, had been collaborating; with Michael Jackson his new friend. The three tracks they recorded at Jackson's home studio were never completed. Freddie would later say that after the success of Thriller, which had taken Jackson where Hot Space had failed to take Queen, 29 million albums sold within one year, the eccentric star simply withdrew and became inaccessible, much to Freddie's dismay. Unofficially, Freddie felt that's the Jacksons had used him somewhat. Freddie also began work on his own solo album, Mr. Bad Guy.

At the end of August, the band reassembled, calmer, still nervous of each other, but ready to work together again — although Freddie had found the record company changes upsetting, and it was only the new deal with Capitol in United States that gave him the impetus to return to the studio — at the Record Plant Studios in Los Angeles. Initially, they had been commissioned to write a film soundtrack, but when the project fell through they began work on their next album, The Works. Freddie's 'Keep Passing the Open Windows', written for the film did make it onto the finished album.

With The Works, everyone wanted to change direction again, and Brian May and Roger Taylor finally managed to return to the rock sound they craved, although John's funk and Freddie's electronic music also got a look in. But there were too many new machines, according to Roger, and the technology ran away with them. Freddie was a fountain of ideas as long as he was concentrating, a period that would now last for perhaps an hour before he would be off and gone.

But when he was concentrating, he helped create two songs on the album that were destined to join the ranks of Queen's great standout tracks; firstly Radio Ga Ga; this one reached number 2 in the UK and was written by Roger Taylor but apparently the drummer wasn't afraid of letting Freddie loose on it during recording; and secondly 'I Want to Break Free', a John Deacon number destined for notoriety thanks to the video in which the lads all dressed in women's clothes, a no 3 hit in the UK. A third was also a success, Brian May's examination of the Cuban missile crisis in 1962, 'Hammer to Fall, a heavy metal track, which got to number 13 in the UK.

Freddie also wrote a top ten hit, and Brian, who had worked closely with the singer on the song, considered "It's a Hard Life' to be the most beautiful song Freddie had ever composed with it's opening line referencing the opera Pagliacci (laugh, clown, at your broken love!). Queen's traditional layered harmonies and piano saw it rise to number 6 in the UK. Perhaps it was, as Brian said, an expression of Freddie's longing for a lasting relationship amidst the temporary lovers, for the sense of permanence, perhaps, that Mary had once given him. The hedonist in Freddie would never allow him to admit it privately, but who could tell what was autobiographical and what wasn't in a song?

Sadly, the bickering had become a constant in their music studio lives and continued through the sessions for the new album. As always, the music was at the core of their arguments and choices and even obstinate Brian would yield to the others decisions, although he would never give up on a composition he had written without a fight. They all knew, after their forays into solo projects that, as many bands had found before, the band was a greater creature then any of its individual members cared to admit; except Freddie, who

RIGHT: Live at the Montreux Rock Festival, 1984

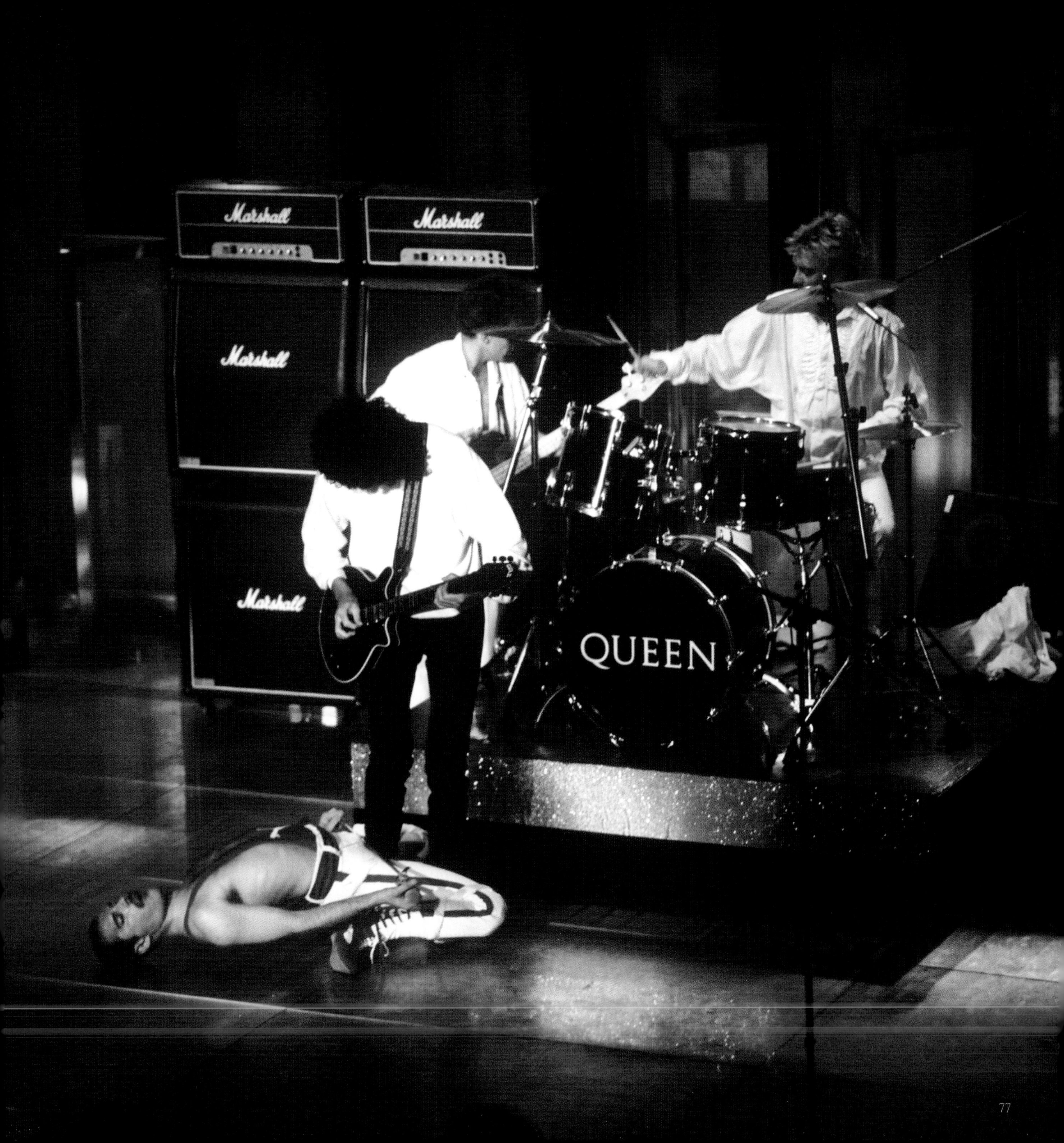
Marshall
Marshall
Marshall
Marshall
Marshall
QUEEN

stated that, "*… without the others I am nothing*".

Queen and producer Mack were, indeed, a royal marriage, bouncing ideas around and never afraid to put them into practice. Even Mack, however, needed a break from the intensity of the studio and would repair to a nude bar across the road with John Deacon to relax. Freddie was determined never to relax, celebrating his 37th birthday with stars such as Elton John in true Freddie style.

The hothouse atmosphere continued when they regrouped in Munich to finish the album, and John Deacon was the first to succumb, flying to Bali to get away from the intensity of the atmosphere in the studio as the sessions continued on into January 1984. Freddie, on the other hand, made his life even more fractured when, besides his current male friend Winnie Kirchberger — another conflicted relationship, fraught with jealous arguments — he met Barbara Valentin, an Australian actress and model and immediately fell in love. Despite the fact that he had "*formed a bond that is stronger than anything I've had with a lover for the last six years*", she encouraged him in his frantically freewheeling lifestyle, and they encouraged each other to consume more drugs, alcohol and sex, together or with others; a disastrous and dangerous downwards spiral of self-indulgence. And Paul Prenter, boasting that he had turned songs into hits and "*trampling*" over everyone including the United States press corps, had created a lot of bad feeling, which everyone wrongly attributed to Freddie. It did serious damage to the group's image in the US.

Fans were given a shot from the new album on the 23rd of January when 'Radio Ga Ga' was released, Roger's blast of nostalgia for the early days before video became so important to music. Finally Roger had a hit, for it struck a chord and the "*arrogant nonsense*", NME again, was soon at number 2 in the UK. An "instant jewel', according to Rolling Stone.

The album itself followed on the 1st of February and also climbed to number two in the UK and was a top 3 in numerous other countries. The Works was, Rolling Stone announced, having been trimmed of the usual excess, "*a royal feast of hard rock without that awful metallic aftertaste*".

In April, it was time for 'I Want to Break Free' to break free and find its way to number 3 in the UK. The video featured of the four guys dressed in women's clothes with Freddie, as always, leading the charge in a leather mini-skirt, a tight pink top and false breasts, plus moustache, was enjoyed by fans all over Europe and Canada, who loved watching the group lampooning themselves. Unlike the Americans, who couldn't conceive what the band was up to, but feared that Freddie might be gay, and some TV stations simply refused to show the video. Fun or not, America was in no mood to laugh; it was the death knell for the band in the US. When the tour started in August, not a single American date had made it onto the schedule that took in Europe, Brazil, Africa, Australia and Japan.

By the time tour started in August, Freddie had completed his first solo album, a pop rock and disco offering that would be released in April, 'Mr. Bad Guy'. It had been a tiring project, because Freddie had included synthesisers and orchestration and was involved in engineering the album as well as performing vocals and playing the piano in the drive to achieve his musical goals. His efforts paid off in the United Kingdom, where the album peaked at number 6. As he was a persona non grata in the US, the album crept guiltily to number 159.

In June, Roger had his second album on the streets, Strange Frontier; it could only reach number 34, and the singles chosen to be detached from the album were singularly unsuccessful.

The inspiration for the set for the tour that confronted the first audience in Belgium on the 24th of August 1984, was a

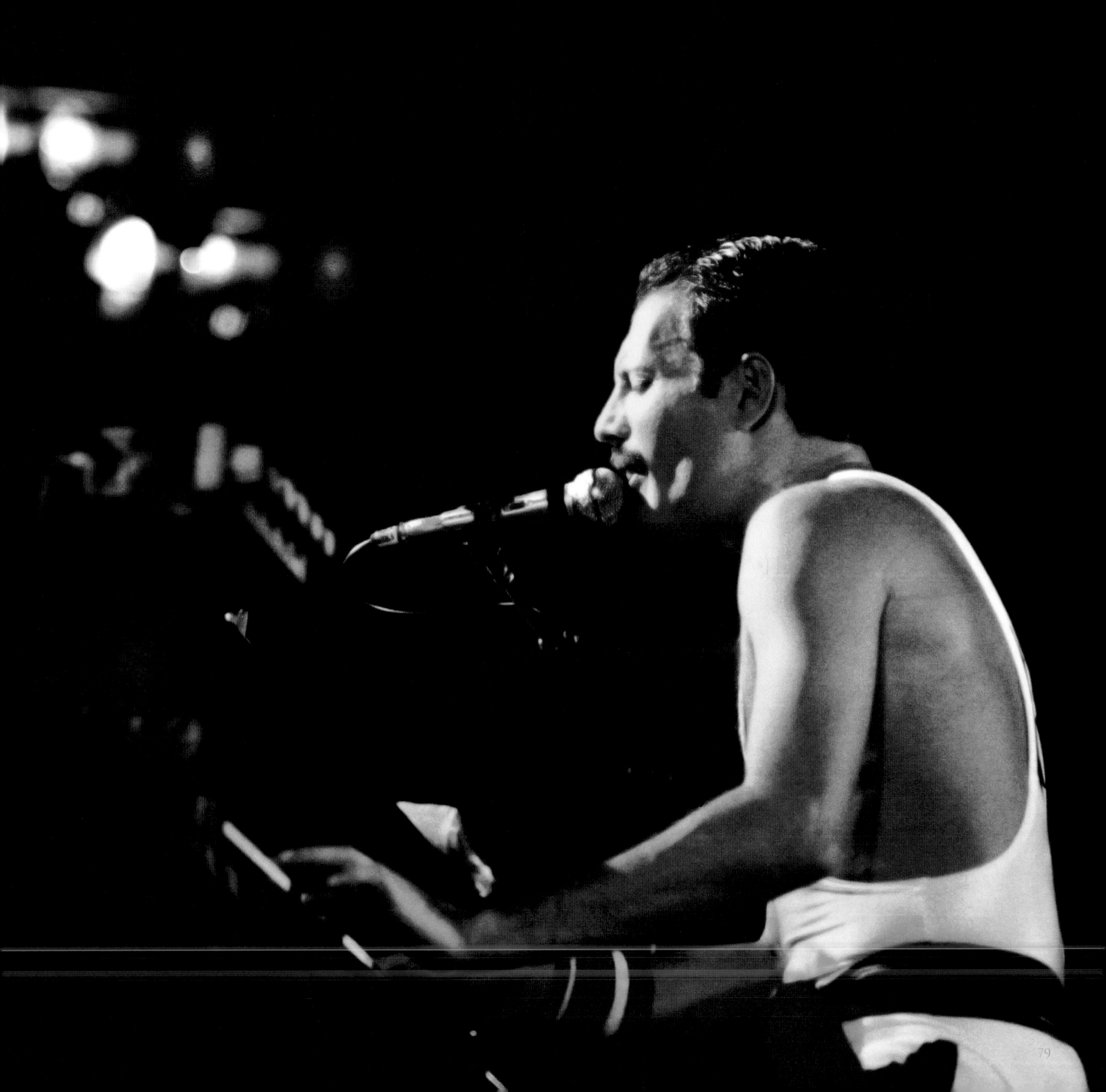

MAIN IMAGE: Queen on stage at the Rock in Rio
festival, Brazil, 1985

MAIN IMAGE: Live in 1985

scene in Fritz Lang's Metropolis; at the rear of the stage there were huge rotating cog-wheels and a cityscape bathed in bright light. There were multiple levels and steps, all of which were a challenge for Freddie, who had damaged a ligament in his knee before the tour started. In Hanover, on the 22nd of September, Mercury took a tumble down the stairs, but decided to continue and was taken to the piano, where he managed to get through three energy laden songs, 'Bohemian Rhapsody', 'We Will Rock You' and 'We Are the Champions', before giving up and going to hospital. That wasn't his only problem; the singer's voice was giving him problems again, but he worried that an operation would change his voice for the worse. And he was under increasing media pressure about his sexual orientation following a story in the Sun newspaper. He felt compelled to continue the denials.

Playing in South Africa, subject at the time to international cultural boycotts and sanctions, earned them no Brownie points, but sold out concerts in Australia and Japan proved no lasting damage had been done.

In January 1985, Queen return to South America to take part in The Rock in Rio Festival, where, with everyone dressed in white, 300,000 people were able to go wild as a tights-clad Freddie Mercury launched into 'Radio Ga Ga', 'Under Pressure' and 'Keep Yourself Alive'. Only when Freddie waltzed onto the stage in a woman's wig and "*plastic falsies*" for 'I Want to Break Free', did it all go slightly pear-shaped; the South Americans had read the song as a cry against dictatorship, and now their vision was being besmirched, and they let that be known with every tin can, stone and anything else they could get their hands on that hurtled towards the stage.

A party later, which Freddie avoided, plagued by old insecurities, was a rock star's joy with drunken dancers and Brian May, of all people, hurling himself into a swimming pool fully clothed. Freddie, apparently, was well supplied by the Machiavellian Paul Prenter with cocaine and boys. His lifestyle visibly spilled over onto the stage; in Auckland New Zealand, the fact that he was suffering from the effects of vodka and port was obvious to the audience.

With the tour over, everyone went their separate ways; Freddie returned to Munich and his complicated web of lovers. Except that there was a new man in his life, one who provided him, finally, with that lasting relationship that Freddie craved; Jim Hutton, a good-looking Irishman, who would later work as Freddie's hairdresser.

Having missed the Band Aid concert of the previous year, Queen were booked to appear at Bob Geldof's next charity enterprise, Live Aid. Queen, would perform two shows in July 1985, once Freddie had agreed after a long period of persuasion. They honed their show with three days of intense rehearsals in North London.

72,000 PEOPLE WERE PRESENT ON THE 13TH OF JULY 1985 IN WEMBLEY STADIUM, 1.9 BILLION AROUND THE WORLD.

Awaiting their slot, Brian was as nervous as a beginner, and Freddie was suffering from a throat infection and had even been diagnosed as too ill to go on stage. He was not looking well. Nonetheless, the musicians went out onto the stage at 6:40 pm and some of their greatest hits had the audience clapping, singing and swearing in unison; the band had, as the press confirmed afterwards, stolen the show from the likes of U2, Status Quo and Spandau Ballet. One of Freddie's sustained notes was later dubbed, "*The Note Heard Round the World*". Brian May probably spoke for the whole band when he said afterwards, perhaps not without justifiable pride, "*I'd never seen anything like that in my life… I'll remember Live Aid till the day I die*".

LIVE AID HAD BREATHED NEW LIFE INTO THE AILING QUEEN.

With this *"shot in the arm"*, the band were re-galvanised, and in September were back in the studio to start work on their 12th album. It was the month of Freddie's 39th birthday, and he partied much as he now lived; as though there were no tomorrow. For Barbara Valentin there wouldn't be; their love affair was over and Freddie would soon be back in London setting up home with Jim Hutton, in a relationship that would last for seven years until Freddie's death, with both men wearing rings as a symbol of their commitment.

Valentin claimed later that she had already noticed the deterioration in her lover's health, including the recurring throat problems, a symptom of HIV, the early symptoms of the disease that would become known as AIDS having first come to the notice of New York doctors in 1981. By October 1985, Rock Hudson had died from the disease. How much Freddie knew about his health is unclear, but in retrospect, friends feel that he might already have known, or at the very least suspected, that he was in danger.

And so a year that had threatened the band's existence ended with them on a musical high note. A Kind of Magic reflected their buoyancy and was hugely successful — and, in retrospect, tinged with sadness, as it turned out to be the last album that would be supported by a concert with Freddie at the front.

And that success came despite the fact that the strange split-up method of working had reached its apotheosis now, with Freddie and John working with Mack alone and Brian and Roger back at Mountain Studios on their own.

Unusually, there were no songs composed solely by Freddie, but each duo were given four songs on the album apiece, with one, 'One Vision' written by all four members of the

LEFT: Performing at the Live Aid concert, Wembley Stadium in London, 13th July 1985

band. Freddie contributed one of his last piano ballads with 'Friends Will Be Friends' written together with Deacon, another rousing Queen anthem that reached number 14 on the UK charts.

A Kind of Magic became an unofficial soundtrack for the film Highlander, and the song 'Princes Of The Universe' was another power track that saw the band back in the heavy-metal and hard-rock mode, and the film became a cult favourite. Also in the film was Brian May's 'Who Wants to Live Forever', which became something of a love theme for the movie; Freddie's soaring and searingly emotional vocals were backed by a full orchestra.

Roger had written the album's eponymous title song 'A Kind of Magic', which did very well in Europe and hit number 3 in the UK. Described by Brian as "*quite lugubrious and heavy*", Freddie had altered Roger's original, adding instrumental breaks and a new baseline, and in wanting to make it more child friendly had changed the song's order. Freddie was right to do so, and it became what one writer called "*one of Queen's purest pop songs*".

The recordings for A Kind of Magic would continue through to April 1986, but en route to its release in June, each member of the band became involved with other projects outside of Queen, before reconvening for two Wembley Stadium concerts, also in June.

Four days after the release of the album on June the 3rd, The Magic Tour was underway in Europe. As the album went speeding on its way to the number 1 spot in the UK, what fans were presented with in Sweden on June the 7th — with Roger having just become a father again, a daughter, Rory — was the biggest and largest concert the band had ever undertaken, seen by more than one million people over its twenty-six European dates; no one could know that it would

be the last tour for nineteen years; and, therefore, the last for Freddie. But Freddie would go out in a blaze of glory clad in a crown and an ermine cloak, a trooper to the end giving the audience and the band every ounce of energy he possessed in a powerful performance full of his characteristic confidence and joie de vivre, joking, strutting, self-deprecating, seemingly unaffected by drink, drugs and cigarettes, living up to his description of Queen shows; "*A concert is not a live rendition of our album. It's a theatrical event*".

In July, they took in four shows in the United Kingdom, two at Wembley Stadium where 150,000 people would watch their heroes perform on the biggest stage ever with inflatable dolls floating above them despite torrential rain during the first show.

The offstage party in celebration of their concerts was as elaborately decadent as ever — "*I like that sort of thing. I like strip clubs and strippers and wild parties*", a quote from Roger — with naked waiters and waitresses, topless models and stars but without Freddie's new live-in partner, Jim Hutton — although, tellingly, and to blind prying eyes, with the ever-loyal Mary Austin.

Queen were pleased to be ahead of the game again when they played a concert in Hungary, the first stadium rock gig behind the Iron Curtain according to EMI, performing to a crowd of 80,000 at the Népstadion in Budapest. It was one of the biggest rock concerts ever held in Eastern Europe. Then it was on to Spain, where Freddie expressed admiration for the opera singer Montserrat Caballé, a remark that would later lead to a collaboration between the two, and then the final concert at Knebworth — Freddie's last concert, which he closed with "*good night and sweet dreams*".

The fractures between the musicians were already quite deep; Freddie announced "*I don't want to do this anymore*", and with the rift between Queen and the US as unbridgeable

RIGHT: Queen arrives at the Knebworth Festival by helicopter, 9th August 1986

as ever, there were no new concert challenges on the horizon.

Reflective John Deacon, too, was displaying distinct signs of stress from the pressure of work, even hurling his bass across the stage at one point, and there was a sense amongst people who knew him that he wasn't far from throwing in the towel. In hindsight, some of Freddie's comments in other ways, not simply interpreted as a desire to stop the roundabout. He was now 40 years old, and gaps were opening up around him as friends succumbed to AIDS. Rumours were already circulating in the press about his own health.

Brian, too, had problems; his marriage was under strain. In 1986, he had met the actress Anita Dobson, and he and Christine finally separated in 1988, plunging Brian into years of depression.

Roger buried himself in work, but as though he, too, were in need of change, an escape from the strain of being in Queen, he formed a new band, The Cross, which, during their six years of existence, released three albums.

Freddie went back to the studio to record another song that would seem to be autobiographical though written for The Platters in 1955; 'The Great Pretender'. The video to accompany the song, which showed Freddie in many of his plethora of stage characters, became one of the best known of his career, and he himself thought it encapsulated his own musical persona, "*I am the great pretender*" he commented. 'The Great Pretender', released in February 1987, reached number 4 in the UK charts.

1987; a landmark year for Freddie. Montserrat Caballé wanted to record with him, so Freddie got down to work on an album of duets with the great opera star. It became their Barcelona album, one of Freddie's greatest;

RELEASED IN OCTOBER 1987, IT WOULD REACH NUMBER 8 IN THE UK CHARTS.

RIGHT: Freddie Mercury and Monserrat Caballe perform Barcelona at KU club Ibiza on May 29, 1987

FROM ELATION TO DESPAIR

The show was over in late April 1987, according to Freddie's partner, Jim Hutton; Freddie's diagnosis was AIDS. Jim refused the singer's offer to end the relationship, telling the star that he wasn't going anywhere and that he loved him. Those closest to him were told, although the band didn't hear the news until later; Freddie didn't want to discuss his condition, which was already beginning to show the first visible signs of itself.

Paul Prenter had been fired sometime before and went to the press with his own wooden spoon to stir things up, and from then on, they would follow Freddie's every move. Whatever Freddie's state of mind, and he continued to deny anything was amiss stating exhaustion as the cause of his increasingly haggard appearance, amidst this growing turmoil he went to perform with Montserrat Caballé on Ibiza. They were given a standing ovation by a star-studded audience, and a top 10 hit single followed.

It was obvious that Freddie was very unwell, and the others were beginning to suspect what it might be. With Freddie's diagnosis still unknown to them at the start of the sessions, apparently, the band decided to continue doing what they did best, make music, and at the beginning of 1988 they went to the studio for the 13th studio album, hopefully entitled, The Miracle. Because of Freddie's decreasing energy levels, it would take a year to make starting in January, the month that Roger married Dominique Beyrand for the sake of the children, before moving in with another woman, model Deborah Leng. Brian had become a father again to daughter Emily early in 1988, although the damage between them had been done and he was soon to leave Christine and move into a house on his own. It wasn't long before he was mourning the death of his father, too. All of these unwanted endings left him mentally disoriented and affected his contribution to the new album; he confessed to spending "*whole days*

sitting there blank, I was in such a depression". He tried to overcome it all by accepting work wherever he could find it outside of Queen.

The band reconvened in London, initially, for the new album in sober mood and agreed that all songs would be credited to the band and that they would all work together in one studio again. Despite his illness, Freddie would yo-yo between recording sessions in London and Mountain Studios in Switzerland and other obligations.

It was January 1989 before work on The Miracle drew to a close. When released in June it was a number 1 hit and even in America it got to number 24, with one review saying that Freddie Mercury's vocals had never sounded better. Press reception was generally favourable for the album filled with "*rock, pop, metal, clever melodies and cunning stylisations*". In retrospect of course, some of the lyrics, particularly in 'Was It All Worth It?', seem searingly poignant in view of what was shortly to take place.

Freddie's life had now been allotted a limited time span, and he was keen to keep creating, although the band, by now informed of what was happening, hadn't intended, or indeed thought that there would be, a follow-up album. But they immediately agreed to make one and started work in session blocks of two or three weeks to accommodate Freddie's reducing energy levels. May and Taylor filled the gaps with as much work as they could.

So March 1989 saw them back in the studios in Switzerland to start work on their 14th studio album, Innuendo. Needless to say, Freddie was a changed man; gone the desire for hedonism in Munich; he bought himself a flat overlooking Lake Geneva. "*For him the studio was an oasis*", said Brian, "*a place where life was just the same as it always had been. He loved making music, he lived for it*".

RIGHT: Freddie Mercury at KU club Ibiza, 1987

In the studio, the boys shared the ideas, and despite Freddie's diminishing vocal power, he still managed to soar over three octaves on tracks that ranged from a harder rock sound to psychedelic effects on 'I'm Going Slightly Mad' and complex musical creations, for the six-and-a-half minutes of the title track, 'Innuendo', for example, which started life as a jam session with Freddie adding lyrics — there was also a true joint effort to polish what May referred to as "*a very strange track... like a fantasy adventure land*", which resulted in another number one hit in the UK.

Eight tracks in total were detached and sent on their way as singles. The most successful was 'These Are the Days of Our Lives', which reached number one in the UK in December 1991. The video for the song proved to be Freddie's last and in retrospect, poignant, if not heart-rending.

As Freddie succumbed more and more to his illness and he needed help to administer the medication, given by Jim Hutton amongst others, recording sessions stretched out until November of 1990. Freddie also told his sister but not his parents; it was hard for his increasingly ravaged form to hide the truth. But the last thing he wanted was the pity of those around him. The press had scented the fox, however, and were merciless in their pursuit, eventually camping permanently outside his home with the other band members closing ranks, unyielding and protecting his privacy.

And still Freddie wanted to continue work, even after the Innuendo sessions had finished, to work until he dropped as he put it. It wasn't easy for him, but he forced himself to sing even difficult sections and was not scared of downing a vodka or two to give himself the push he needed to succeed.

Paul Prenter had died from AIDS related complications; Jim Hutton had also been diagnosed with the disease, although he wouldn't tell Freddie for some time, not wanting to heighten the singer's distress.

Freddie continued to record, at his own insistence, and so his bandmates did, too. One of the songs was 'Mother Love', which is thought to be his last recording with words that are unbearably poignant; "*I can't take it if you see me cry, I long for peace before I die.*" He, was, said Brian, "*without fear, really*".

When the new album was released in February 1991, it went to number 1 in the UK, a fitting send off for Farrokh Bulsara and his alter ego Freddie Mercury. By the middle of 1991 as the illness worsened, Freddie had retired to his Kensington home. And then, in November, he decided he had had enough; he stopped taking his medication.

HE HAD DECIDED TO DIE.

On the 23rd, Freddie released a statement to the press. Now the world would know. But by the time most people found out it was all over. By the evening of the 24th November, Freddie had gone.

No more "*crazy shopping*" as the Japanese used to say with glee at his spending sprees, no more crowns, no more energy-pumped displays of pure, joyful creativity.

HIS FELLOW BANDMATES WERE IN SHOCK.

Queen had risen to the dizzying peaks of pop music success, driven on by their kaleidoscopic lead singer, one of the most talented and innovative singers of his generation, a skilled performer, a showman par excellence, abrasive and gentle, a man torn apt by the twin snakes of wealth and fame.

And as Roger Taylor once said of the glittering presence that was Freddie Mercury, "*He was the best — no one could touch him*". His technique was breathtaking and saturated with musicality, his ability to phrase, to turn the tempo on a

sixpence, his talent to effortlessly soar between octaves, was second to none. In the opinion of Roger Daltrey, lead singer of The Who, Freddie was *"the best virtuoso rock 'n' roll singer of all time. "I won't be a rock star, I will be a legend,"* May recalls Freddie saying. He made sure that he was.

Freddie left his home to the friend who had been loyal to him through everything, Mary Austin. Others, including Jim Hutton, benefited in similar ways from Freddie's generosity.

The final album including Freddie, Made in Heaven, cut together from those draining final sessions, was released in 1995 and was likewise a number 1 hit in the UK. So, too, was a version of 'Somebody to Love', which Freddie had made with George Michael.

An extraordinary journey for the band had come to an end. Understandably, it was hard for them to stop, to abandon the vestiges of the taste of fame and adulation Queen had brought them. So, even though there could never be another Freddie Mercury, the three remaining members of the band decided to continue, both as solo performers and later as Queen.

John Deacon decided that it was all over for him, too, in 1997, and his departure further fractured the old lineup.

At the end of 2004, Paul Rogers was invited to join the group, which was now billed as Queen and Paul Rogers, an arrangement that lasted until 2009. From 2011, Adam Lambert began to sing with the band, and the projects they worked on together became known as Queen and Adam Lambert.

Queen's influence on the pop the world was incredibly wide-ranging, with artists as disparate as Robbie Williams and Lady Gaga, Iron Maiden and Judas Priest, Michael Jackson and George Michael quoting them as inspiration. Queen was an extraordinary constellation of individual talents, and their lead singer was not afraid to take their sometimes outlandish ideas to the world wrought into incomparable musical experiences by his own volcanic and chameleon-like personality.

In 2018, the group were presented with a Grammy Lifetime Achievement Award. Freddie would surely have feigned his characteristic hauteur; "But of course, darling!" he might have said, secretly delighted at the recognition of his unique talent and the love that the success represented to Farrokh and his mates Brian, Roger and John, who once got together to play in a band that they dared to call, Queen.

DISCOGRAPHY

ALBUMS

TITLE	RELEASE DATE	CHART POSITION
Queen	13th of July 1973	UK 24 / US 83
Queen II	8th of March 1974	UK 5 / US 49
Sheer Heart Attack	8th of November 1974	UK 2 / US 12
A Night at the Opera	21st of November 1975	UK 1 / US 4
A Day at the Races	10th of December 1976	UK 1 / US 5
News of the World	28th of October 1977	UK 4 / US 3
Jazz	10th of November 1978	UK 2 / US 6
The Game	27th of June 1980	UK 1 / US 1
Flash Gordon	8th of December 1980	UK 10 / US 23
Hot Space	3rd of May 1982	UK 4 / US 22
The Works	27th of February 1984	UK 2 / US 23
A Kind of Magic	2nd of June 1986	UK 1 / US 46
The Miracle	22nd of May 1989	UK 1 / US 24
Innuendo	5th of February 1991	UK 1 / US 30
Made in Heaven	6th of November 1995	UK 1 / US 58

SINGLES

YEAR / TITLE	CHART POSITION
1973	
Keep Yourself Alive	
1974	
Liar	
Seven Seas of Rhye	UK 10
Killer Queen	UK 2 / US 12
1975	
Now I'm Here	UK 11
Keep Yourself Alive (re-issue)	US 89
Bohemian Rhapsody	UK 1 / US 9

DISCOGRAPHY

Year / Title	Chart Position
1976	
You're My Best Friend	UK 7 / US 16
Somebody to Love	UK 2 / US 13
1977	
Tie Your Mother Down	UK 31 / US 54
Good Old-Fashioned Lover Boy	UK 17
Teo Torriatte (Let Us Cling Together)	
Long Away	
We Are the Champions / We Will Rock You	UK 2 / US 4
1978	
Spread Your Wings	UK 34
It's Late	US 74
Bicycle Race / Fat Bottomed Girls	UK 11 / US 24
1979	
Don't Stop Me Now	UK 9 / US 86
Jealousy	
Mustapha	
Love of My Life	UK 63
We Will Rock You (live)	
Crazy Little Thing Called Love	UK 2 / US 1
1980	
Save Me	UK 11
Play the Game	UK 14
Another One Bites the Dust	UK 7
Need Your Loving Tonight	
Flash	UK 10
1981	
Under Pressure (with David Bowie)	UK 1
1982	
Body Language	UK 25 / US 19

DISCOGRAPHY

YEAR / TITLE	CHART POSITION
Life is Real	US 57
Las Palabras de Amor (The Words of Love)	UK 17
Calling All Girls	US 40
Put out the Fire	US 15
Staying Power	
Back Chat	UK 40
1984	
Radio Ga Ga	UK 2 / US 22
I Want to Break Free	UK 3
It's a Hard Life	UK 6
Hammer to Fall	UK 13 / US 57
Tear It Up	US 52
Thank God It's Christmas	UK 21
1985	
One Vision	UK 7 / US 19
1986	
A Kind of Magic	UK 3
Princes of the Universe	
Friends Will Be Friends	UK 14
Pain Is So Close to Pleasure	
Who Wants to Live for Ever	UK 24
One Year of Love	
1989	
I Want It All	UK 3 / US 3
The invisible Man	UK 12
Scandal	UK 25
The Miracle	UK 21
1991	
Innuendo	UK 1 / US 17
I'm Going Slightly Mad	UK 22
Headlong	UK 14 / US 3

DISCOGRAPHY

YEAR / TITLE	CHART POSITION
The Show Must Go on	UK 16 / US 40
Bohemian Rhapsody / These are the Days of Our Lives	UK 1 / US 16
1992	
Who Wants to Live for Ever (re-release)	
We Will Rock You / We Are the Champions (live/studio)	
1995	
Heaven for Everyone	UK 2
A Winter's Tale	UK 6
1996	
I Was Born to Love You	
Too Much Love Will Kill You	UK 15
Let Me Live	UK 9
You Don't Fool Me	UK 17
1997	
No One But You (Only the Good Die Young) /	
Tie Your Mother Down	UK 13
Under Pressure	UK 14
2000	
Princes of the Universe (re-release)	
2003	
We Will Rock You (re-release)	
Another One Bites the Dust / We Will Rock You (re-release)	
2010	
Keep Yourself Alive / Stone Cold Crazy	
2014	
Let Me in Your Heart Again	UK 102

DISCOGRAPHY

LIVE ALBUMS

TITLE	RELEASE DATE	CHART POSITION
Live Killers	22nd of June 1979	UK 3 / US 16
Live Magic	4th of December 1989	UK 5
At the Beeb	4th of December 1989	UK 67
Live at Wembley '86	26th of May 1992	UK 2 / US 53
Queen on Fire - Live at The Bowl	4th of November 2004	UK 20
Queen Rock Montréal	29th of October 2007	UK 20
Hungarian Rhapsody: Queen Live in Budapest	20th of September 2012	
Live Back the Rainbow '74	8th of September 2014	UK 11 / US 66
A Night at the Odeon Hammersmith 1975	20th of November 2015	UK 40
On Air	4th of November 2016	UK 25

COMPILATION ALBUMS

TITLE	RELEASE DATE	CHART POSITION
Greatest Hits	26th of October 1981	UK 1 / US 14
Greatest Hits II	28th of October 1991	UK 1
Classic Queen	10th of March 1992	US 4
The 12th collection	1992	
Queen Rocks	3rd of November 1997	UK 7
Greatest Hits III	9th of November 1999	UK 5
Stone Cold Classics	11th of April 2006	
The A-Z of Queen Volume 1	10th of July 2007	
Absolute Greatest	16th of November 2009	UK 3 / US 195
Deep Cuts, Volume 1 (1973-1976)	14th of March 2011	UK 92
Deep Cuts, Volume 2 (1977-1982)	27th of June 2011	UK 175
Deep Cuts, Volume 3 (1984-1995)	5th of September 2011	UK 155
Icon	11th of June 2013	
Queen Forever	10th of November 2014	UK 5 / US 38